AF380321

BORUT LESJAK

ONE MOON PRESENT

A Radical Healing Formula to Transform Your Life in 28 Days

STUDIO ◆ BLEST

ONE MOON PRESENT
A Radical Healing Formula to Transform Your Life in 28 Days
Love Yourself Through Hard Emotions and Hard Times
By Borut Lesjak

LOVE YOURSELF THROUGH series, book 2

www.onemoonpresent.com
www.borutlesjak.com

Cover illustration and design by Ksenija Konvalinka
Cover photo by Gregor Kresal
Interior art by Darja Klančar
Edited by Sarah Berti

Publisher's Cataloging-in-Publication
(Provided by National and University Library, Slovenia)

LESJAK, Borut, 1971-
One moon present: a radical healing formula to transform your life in 28 days : love yourself through hard emotions and hard times / by Borut Lesjak. - Srednja vas : Studio Blest, 2020. - (Love yourself through series ; book 2)

ISBN 978-961-7100-51-8

ONE
MOON
PRESENT

The Moon.
A round reflection.

Father Sun sends his love to Mother Earth and Moon is the sacred messenger:
Golden light transmutes to silver.
Moon descends to our hearts:
Silver light transmutes to rainbow.

Night shivers and looks. Air bites alive. Heavens arch in awe.
I am moon bathed, I am an inner smile, I am yes.
In my heart: a trip, a luna story, a blue-veined cycle.
Pause to re-wild.

The world is oh so Real.

Listen to the soundless whiff of impending death.
Upon me this shining, shuddering moment. Yellow crescent evanescence.
Soft like moonlit nights, silvertender knee to soil surrender.
Worlds created, lunar ballad, realms destroyed.

What mystery, this bloom bared life! This glowing universe!
Love tree glinting with we and web.
Birth or moon or sol or I who in-verse the shine.
Luminous in part-time presence.

Moonlight, a dream message.
I, a Messenger, Interpreter, Translating Spirit wind.
To Humanity's ink.

I am the Reflection round.
The Moon.

My deepest gratitude flows to my dear friend David Elliott, author, teacher, and healer, with whom I've studied this work for many years. I borrowed many ideas and tools from him, as well as others, in the creation of this book.

David, I am forever thankful for the second chance you helped me seize in this lifetime, and for being an immense inspiration for self-love, undivided attention, dedication, kindness, grounding, and humor.

Contents

Introduction

I trust love.

In this life, I have experienced hard emotions and hard times. At the time, I didn't know better than to suffer. In the process, I learned a healing method based on self-love—an element I wasn't intimately familiar with before.

I chose healing.

From the pits of powerlessness, abuse, confusion, resistance, denial, self-invalidation, and despair, I paved a joyful path to awakening and expansion into a more complete human being. Daily, I now embrace and love myself through all emotions and circumstances, faithfully following the guiding star of my purpose.

Life is good.

I've been called to show up and give forward this spark of inspiration I've been honored to receive from many beings, energies, Mother Earth, and Spirit. For someone who used to tremble and blush when speaking in public, I've come a long way. I lead healing events and write books.

This book is for you.

I firmly believe the healing method and tools which helped me, can help others too. Drawing on years of experience and intuition, I devised a simple yet radical healing formula that can transform your view of life in 28 days: ONE MOON PRESENT. If you're willing to trust love too, you are ready!

The choice is yours.

I. START HERE:
What's in this book for you?

Welcome aboard

Do you want to feel better in your life? Do you want to experience well-being, health, joy, peace, and love every day as a rule, not as an exception?

If your answer is yes, a potent and pragmatic healing formula I call ONE MOON PRESENT is for you.

My name is Borut Lesjak and I'll be your guide through your hard emotions and hard times into self-love if you care to join me on this adventure. I'll share my journey with you, the insights and visions I've created along the way. I humbly hope to move you so you can find your own trust, courage, and strength of love necessary to open up to the infinite within. It is waiting for you.

At first I was guided to create this as a short booklet, merely a companion to a very powerful tool: an ancient Eastern pranayama breathwork meditation. This meditation lies at the core of the healing work I use. It will help you generate the self-love and presence you need to live through anything negative and transmute it to the experience of being alive.

But as I wanted to formulate the work with a whole string of components all taking part in our healing, I realized it was not for me to say which are more and which are less important. So the intent of the book shifted and its content grew.

This book will present you with the tools that have been waiting, dormant within you, for eons and generations, probably tucked inside your DNA and racial memory. You will decide which of them are suitable for you at this stage of the game and how you will choose to apply them.

Remember, the choice is yours alone!

This book is unique

Why would I say that? Because *you* are reading this line *right now*! You might have felt a tingling sensation while reading that. That's exactly the kind of presence and energy we will work with.

Make no mistake: the power is in you, right here and now. I take no credit for it.

Can you *feel* it, this power? Yes, you can—if you choose. It is your *chi*, your life force, your spirit, or your soul, as it vibrates through your being! It's your *awareness*. And now you are *conscious* of it.

This book aims to deal with awareness and other seemingly spiritual matters in an utterly pragmatic way. That's why it might be unique as well, or at least somewhat *different*. You and I both trust some higher power to seal the deal and bring the much needed, sought-for healing into your life, restoring flow and balance on your command. The rest will happen by itself.

As we will soon find out, it doesn't have to be hard.

Now, if you are a super-curious and active person, you can safely vault directly to the practical part of the book—if you haven't already. Why, you can even test the included breathwork meditation at this link: **freemeditation14.onemoonpresent.com** without any further introduction. I encourage you to go ahead if that's how you roll. That's exactly what I did when I first encountered this method.

But if you want to tread softly and learn more before you jump into the water, read on.

What you will get out of this book

My commitment and promise to you is this: if you honestly lean in, open up, suspend your judgment, and give this work a fair chance you *will* experience a change in your life.

Either you can simply create some peace in your day and let go of stress and fatigue, or you can certainly learn to live fully in the presence of negativity (your own or the collective's). Or, you can go as deep as you want and bring about lasting results that mean all the difference to your purpose for being alive.

What makes me qualified to say this?

I've been born a sensitive, highly intuitive individual. My gift is *claircognizance*, which means I just know things without knowing how. Before I come across as arrogant or in any way special, please, bear with me as I express my opinion that each and every one of us has been born intuitive. We never lose the ability but we often mislay the trust in it. Yet the good news is that we can reclaim it whenever we want.

For decades, I've been *exchanging* with the work of healing in many practical forms. I've learned about the undeniable capacity of human beings to heal automatically as soon as we *step out of our own way*.

There is no doubt in my mind: when we consciously and consistently choose to heal, we do. It doesn't even matter if we're not sure what *healing* is—but you know what I'm talking about, don't you?

Whether you are afraid of pain, or shame, or financial obligation, or responsibility around raising children, or being a good parent or partner or simply a good person, whether you worry about your future or feel sad about your past, whether you're angry with your neighbors or can't abide the politics—whatever trouble is making your life miserable at this stage, and if you feel stuck or have been feeling stuck for a long time—there just may be a real way out.

I must tell you this, though: from what I perceive as part of our present human condition, there is a powerful interplay between what we resist and where we are stuck in life. I'm talking about our convictions, beliefs, and expectations. We can get stubborn there and normally we do. That's not a random coincidence. An energetic link of a cause/effect lies behind it, one that is hard to see and believe, because it's all so circular.

But when we ultimately get bored with our old story and sincerely feel the pull of freedom, when we can already smell the fresh scent of a new dream coming true, and when we choose to heal—as I already said—we do.

If you can sense the truth in these words you're more than ready. And this book with all its tools and exercises will gently guide you to rekindle your own light and trust the compass of your soul once more.

Is this book for you?

Let's do a quick test: are you afraid?

I'd like you to pause here and take your time. This book is not something you want to absorb quickly and then tick a checkbox: *done.* If you are sincere in your desire to deal with any hard emotion or to heal something else in your life, we will go slowly, patiently, and focus on what is of the essence. In this case: your emotions and feelings.

So, are you afraid? Feel it! Feel it in your body, in your nervous system, or in your energy field. I know you're trying to think it out, and that's okay. We're all wired and programmed that way. This book will deal with reprogramming, or deprogramming.

If your fear feels too big and scary at this moment and you simply can't go there—that's perfectly okay too. I promise you we'll learn to use a special formula that can help you with that. In fact, that is exactly what this book is about. Do you want to be patient and ask your heart to create more trust? I know you can do that: our hearts *can* do that!

You can simply draw a deep breath here, no matter what you feel. Focus on your chest opening up and filling with life-giving air. When you exhale, relax and let go of too much control. Find that trust in your heart. It might be glowing or tingling there, within. You can even smile.

If you're ready to feel more, please continue reading. Or, you can skip this section for now and we'll just make a quick note that we hit the wall here. We were looking for that, so: good work. You can just leaf through the book or read one of my sample stories in the last chapter. They are based on real events in my life. And when you decide it's time for you to move forward through negativity, you can give a chance to breathwork meditation. It's simple, gentle, and awesome!

You can access the meditation for free at this link:
freemeditation14.onemoonpresent.com.

What *do* you fear? (Pause and feel it.)
What do you fear *the most*?
How are you coping with your fears?
Are you fighting, are you waging a war against your fear?
Does that make you sad or angry?
Frustrated?
Confused?
Exhausted?
All of the above?

I invite you to take your notebook or open a document on your computer now and write all this down. I suggest that you do that because I believe it can make a difference. Writing can focus and ground us. It can help you go deeper into your feelings and trust what you feel. It might bring you more clarity. And while you're writing, you might catch a glimpse of self-love: the sense that "you are there for you." You might deeply realize that it's all good—much better than you would believe when you focus on just the negative.

Do you want to get your life back? If you feel stuck and powerless to change anything long term, I promise you there is a gentle way out: *through*.

This book will get you started. The fact that you're reading this tells me that this book is for you and that you're ready and willing to do some lifting—which doesn't have to be heavy. But it will be work and you will be the one doing the work, and that will make all the difference. Why?

Because in the process, you will regain your self-confidence. You will regain the trust that you *can* make a change after all. You'll viscerally realize that you have it in you—that you always did—and now you will have pulled it off. You will have done it! And you will learn to respect and love yourself in ways you didn't know were possible.

And that is just the beginning. I assure you, there will come a turning point in your life when you'll deeply sense better times are coming—*to stay*! You will rekindle your hope once more.

What secrets lie in there?

When I say "in there" I mean not only this book, I mean *you*. I ask for your permission to guide you to find your inner compass because only you can do that. I believe we're all extremely powerful beings and ultimately only we can sabotage ourselves—nobody else can do that to us. So the good news is: if you got yourself into a mess you can get yourself out as well!

I did my best to keep this book as simple and direct as possible. I start with this introductory chapter, START HERE, which has an important role in reminding you that you are still here, that you still nurture your trust. You haven't given up yet! As long as you don't, there is a chance. As long as we breathe, there is a chance.

Chapter Two, BRIEFING, will offer some simple guidelines that might prove important to the mind. Since the mind is probably calling the shots at this point in your life, it's vital to keep it informed and invite it to play along in a friendly way. And once you connect the dots and create the balance between all aspects of your being—physical, emotional, mental, as well as spiritual—you'll have stepped into your power and will be able to better listen to your intuition. It will unerringly tell you what is what. You'll be creating your own best-suited, personal theory in no time.

Chapter Three, ONE MOON PRESENT, is the core of the book, with detailed descriptions of the most important tools I'm using on my own path of healing and in my healing work with others. I draw from personal experience and the work I write about has been thoroughly tested in practice.

Recently, I've been intuitively guided to organize the daily, routine tasks of self-healing into a concise and easy-to-follow, pragmatic formula. I received a poetic name for it: *One Moon Present*. It is the central point of this work and also of the *Love*

Yourself Through series of books, which address specific areas of healing: fear, anger, sadness, and others.

And the last chapter, ENGAGE, will provide you with a sampling of real-life examples of the application of the ONE MOON PRESENT formula. It will impress upon you the final instruction and inspiration to do your work, and see you off.

I envision our "engagement" more as a playground, a playing ground, rather than a proving ground or even a battleground. I stress that because I realize so many self-help methods are based on harsh discipline and rigorous, rigid rules one has to follow to the letter to get the ultimate reward—the healing—and I simply don't buy that. The more we remain relaxed, creative, and inspired, the softer our stuck emotions and the stronger our restorative flow of energy will become. After all, the core of what we're learning here is *self-love.*

On the other hand, we *will* be shifting things for real, so roll up your sleeves. We'll be conducting a grounded, sober, common-sense process of finding our truth and worth within. Moreover, we'll effectively learn how to generate our well-being ourselves. If that sounds preposterous to you—well, maybe that's where some of your beliefs might be a bit stuck. But perhaps that's exactly why you're reading this now. So let's get going! Are you game?

I'll share with you some of my most intimate moments of hard emotions. A tiny collection of real stories will not only help you identify with me but entice you to open up to your own stories of a similar nature and get in touch with your emotions and feelings. You'll witness how a commitment to a daily meditation can gradually change your life—from hell to heaven, as it was in my case. Each story is an anecdote, an invocation, and it doesn't aim to indoctrinate you or ask you to relinquish your precious power in any way.

In fact, my message to you is that we're not so different at all. We *are* in the same boat. What happened to me perhaps happened to everyone at some point. Is it happening to you, too? You'll see. The patterns behind the stories are abstract and universal. And the agents that seem to be causing our suffering are impersonal. That's what I claim and I'll do my best to illustrate my point. No need to fight anything. Strife only begets more strife.

What we need is a safe place within, where we can rebuild our foundations, and grow our roots from and into the reality of Mother Earth and everyday life.

How it all started for me

I sincerely believe this book can change your life. Not the book—*you* will change your life if you apply the exercises and commit to doing your work daily, if possible. I believe that because that's what happened to me. I'm talking from experience.

Eight years ago, I was at rock bottom. I had no hope. I had no energy to even want to help myself. Every day was black and gray. Pain, hurt, guilt, unworthiness, helplessness. When I lost my dream job, was diagnosed with diabetes, and got divorce papers in the mail, I thought I would die. But I didn't.

With nothing to lose, I followed my intuition to a website of one David Elliott whom I had heard about for the first time a year earlier from a friend of mine. I clicked on the recording of the pranayama breathwork meditation and tried a couple of breaths. In one single, fateful instant, I knew this was it! I proceeded to read the introduction to David's second book, *Healing*, which was freely available on his website. I loved his style of writing. I hadn't known it was possible to express so much self-love through words. I read on.

A week or so later, I purchased David's 23-minute breathwork meditation called *The Future Beyond 2012*. Yes, the year was 2012 then, and I was pretty scared about my life. I feared the world might be coming to an end as many people claimed. I laid down to breathe and within minutes, something momentous happened.

My heart opened!

Not literally, of course. Some would say my heart chakra opened. All I knew was that everything was melting away within me. My emotions got unstuck, my blocks softened and collapsed, my flow of energy was restored. I cried like a baby and released my sorrow, my problems, my whole personal hell.

After I got up, I wiped away my tears and strolled into the living room. I smiled at my wife and our kids. I was beaming. I wasn't afraid any longer. All of my hopes and dreams were alive and shiny again. My life had only just begun.

The road to healing

That day when my heart first opened after a long time, I made a conscious choice: I chose the healing. I wanted it! I would never return to the dark and damp dungeon of my lack of love in life. I had learned that love can be generated in my heart. No more seeking it elsewhere in vain.

The new hope and passion never left me again, but I must admit that the hard days didn't just go away for good. Hardship and problems kept coming at me—and I kept breathing! I'm talking about breathwork meditation: the single most potent tool I've ever worked with.

During the eight years of my practicing and teaching breathwork, I've come to realize that meditation, in general, can be highly beneficial in anybody's life. Well, that's an understatement. I firmly believe that true meditation is the only thing that can help us develop our awareness and overcome the unconscious denial that stands between hell and heaven on Earth.

By true meditation I mean a consistent and dedicated practice of grounding, relaxing and letting go of the mind, and opening up to faith and your soul entering your body—something I routinely sense as a powerful and pleasant vibration during my breathwork practice. And that's it. That's all we'll ever need to break free.

Once such a healing process becomes a part of our lives, we learn to appreciate its full, lasting, and sustainable value. Like we eat and drink daily, we go to sleep, we wash frequently, we take care of our bodies—we know everything in life needs responsible maintenance—and in the same way we want to meditate on a regular basis. By doing this, we keep clearing our energy and releasing our emotional blocks, we develop our consciousness to stay present easier and more, and we learn about self-love and create our joy and fun in everyday life.

And remember, your healing can be easy.

So, what *is* healing, anyway?

## II.	BRIEFING:

Healing is not rocket science

How much theory do we need?

Not much really. Oftentimes the mind craves information but at a certain point we know enough and it's time to act, to do the work.

I will do my best to keep this book, and specifically this chapter, as concise as possible. My intention is to provide you with just enough theory to help your mind play along without much fuss. After you do some of the practical work with the tools and experience healing first-hand, the path will lead you to wherever you want. The choice is always yours.

For those of you who will feel the call to immerse deeper as a practitioner and perhaps a teacher as well, there are and will be other books available with in-depth explanations—please check at the back of this book for more information.

In this chapter, we'll briefly address how I intuitively and experientially understand feelings, emotions, thoughts, awareness, free will, creativity, self-love, and healing—and especially how it all ties together.

Feel free to skip the theory and jump to practice.

If you feel impatient, you can skip or skim over the theory. I provide a condensed summary at the end of each of the longer sections. Or, you can consult the *Glossary* at the back of the book whenever a term or a concept you encounter doesn't ring a bell.

Again, I firmly believe that what matters is doing the work and all the theory is only a decoy for the mind to quiet down and let us go straight to the business of healing, which is always spiritual in essence.

Note that some of my views may appear surprisingly different from the mainstream knowledge. But I will let you be the judge of what is what, trusting your own intuition and experience, if you choose to give this book and its tools a fair test run. I invite you to reserve your judgment for the time being and open up to the unknown within, preparing some free, fresh space needed to seed and grow your own answers in the process.

Should we fear and fight negative emotions?

No. Not if we want to emerge from the vicious circle of suffering in our life.

Emotions are energy, and all energy is just that: energy. There is no positive or negative energy.

Why do some emotions feel bad, then?

Everything in our experience feels bad when we resist it, when we fight it, or when we run away from it. We define what bad is. Prior to that, all is purely subjective and relative.

But how does that help you in the real world? Nobody wants to feel bad or suffer.

We'll get back to that. That's the point of the book: long-term, lasting healing.

> No negativity needed, no positivity required.

Many self-help recipes I know may wreak more havoc than actual help. They focus on the immediate gratification of erasing or denying the negative. I've often seen "negative" emotions demonized, just like the mind and the ego. But we're here for the long haul.

All feelings, emotions, and thoughts are valid. Whatever rough patch you may have been experiencing in your life that led you to open this book, we'll address it in the context of your choice and your healing.

What I propose and offer tools for is this: let's get clear about what is what first. We'll use the breathwork meditation to pause our fears or stress, and relax, regroup, and restore our energy, which is crucial if we want to build ourselves a foundation we can rely on long term.

It's easy to find a momentary distraction and forget about our problems for a short while, but we all know they will come back to haunt us with a redoubled force. But when we learn how to depend on ourselves and how to use and trust our intuition, and especially when we soak everything we do with self-love—using anything that is happening to us externally or internally as fuel for more self-love—then we're on the right track to creating a healthy and lasting solution to our problems.

So bear with me for now, please, and just ask yourself: *can I suspend my judgment until I try the tools he is talking about, put it all to practice and experience it on my own terms*? If you can, I promise you, there is something for you in this work.

You are not your mind—so who are you?

The thinking mind

Who are you? I often say this is a trick question. Perhaps we are too complex, multi-layered, and infinitely nuanced, and the definition of who we are may depend on our viewpoint. Perhaps it's a matter of where we focus our attention, and how.

It might be easier to define who you are not. And for the purposes of this book and your healing process, I'll claim that you're not your mind. We'll soon connect the dots to see why that plays such an important role on our path to completeness and fulfilment.

Can you pause your thoughts? Can you stop thinking for a while?

If you just did that and you're presently thinking about the complete lack of thoughts in your mind—well… think again.

> Do you think you're not thinking?

I believe it takes a lot of practice and talent to stop thinking altogether. We may need to learn a whole other mode of existence to be able to do that.

But I also believe that we don't really have to stop thinking in order to heal ourselves or improve the quality of our lives. It suffices that we learn to observe our thoughts and cease to identify with them.

Awareness and consciousness

You can try a simple exercise: catch the next thought that comes to you, right now. Simply observe it. It doesn't matter if you judge it or try to suppress it. The mere act of noticing it and becoming aware of it, is all we want here. Also, it doesn't matter what the thought was.

I ask you only this: *who* is observing your thoughts?

In a way, the answer to that is also the answer to the question *who are you?* It's what I call *awareness*. When you pause your ordinary, auto-pilot reactions to whatever comes to and through your mind, and focus on your own process of thinking, you may become aware that *you* exist outside of your mind and thoughts. I call that *consciousness*: being aware of your awareness, or focusing your awareness on itself.

Awareness is basic knowing of the world around you and the attention to it.

Consciousness is sublime, divine awareness of being aware, a state of being awakened or enlightened, a non-linear presence with all there is, externally and internally.

Awareness is a direct consequence of our five senses at work, complemented with our feelings, emotions, and mental processes. It is subject to programming, confusion, denial, resistance—all of which leads to the loss of, or the lessening of the ebb of consciousness.

Consciousness is independent of all of the above. It is unknowable and can't be controlled in any way. It can only be inspired. Consciousness can be raised, developed, and trained almost like a muscle—but not exactly. For what we can train is only the potential for consciousness: we can only seed and water the ground, and patiently wait, perhaps brood, and intend our awakening into a temporarily expanded consciousness.

Sometimes, I use the term *presence* interchangeably with *consciousness*, although I prefer to say *present* rather than *conscious* in the context of an everyday situation. They mean the same: being aware, with clarity and neutrality, not only of the external but also the internal circumstances, such as our feelings, emotions, thoughts, and also our responses to them.

You are unknowable.

Why do I talk about this?

I believe most of our problems are more imagined and mind-created than real. I'm not saying that all the problems are made up. If you take a nasty fall and break your leg, that's pretty real. It's good to acknowledge it and find a grounded way to fix the problem and mend the broken bone.

This book and the ONE MOON PRESENT formula will help you deal with the problems that are a direct consequence of diminished consciousness. By that, I mean being lost in the various identifications with your mental processes, or with your emotions and feelings, as we'll discuss in the next section.

How do we develop and nurture our consciousness to grow—and by doing that, help ourselves decipher, unmask, or overcome many of our mind-created problems?

Strangely enough, there is no need to talk about the process of disidentification. In fact, it might prove to be even counterproductive to address it verbally and mentally. I find that by far the most direct and efficient approach to developing consciousness is *acting*, not thinking. The ONE MOON PRESENT formula incorporates all the necessary elements for that, as we'll see in the next chapter.

ONE MOON PRESENT practice has a way of bringing in more awareness and opening us up to more clarity, or consciousness, by relaxing, pausing, or temporarily neutralizing the mind's control in a healthy, creative manner, by our choice.

If this section feels confusing to you, that's okay. You don't need to understand all of this to create healing in your life. It's optional and you can safely skip to the next chapter and do some practical work.

Summary

To summarize this section: our essence is pure awareness and life is a process of steadily soaking our body in it. The mind is a complex energetic organ of perception with the capacity of creating virtual reality on top of true reality. Still only learning the nature of the mind and how to use it, we get confused easily and mistake the two: awareness and thoughts. Consciousness, or presence, is clarity about what is what on the level of awareness, not thoughts. And expanding consciousness ultimately leads us to healing and to a more real, balanced, and fulfilling life.

How do you feel about your emotions?

Emotions and feelings

There are three subjects I want to address specifically while talking about emotions: the distinction between emotions and feelings, states of being, and mood. These concepts are key to the healing method I use.

Let's start by pointing out the difference between our bodily feelings and emotions. For example, fear is an emotion, but the rush of adrenaline or a clamp in the pit of your stomach is a bodily feeling that accompanies the emotion.

When we face a difficult situation—especially in our tender age—our being may employ a coping mechanism called *denial* that protects our frail ego from being overwhelmed and possibly damaged. Emotions too harsh may be swept "under the rug," or in more technical terms, into the subconsciousness, to be processed and expressed at a later, more convenient time or in a safer space.

The problems occur when we keep suppressing our emotions for too long. We could say our emotions get stuck—and *we* get stuck with them. The balance and natural course of our choices, trajectories and lives get deranged, and we're not even aware of that. From our viewpoint, everything is just fine, until the body signals us a red alert by way of pain, sickness or chronic illness.

There is a powerful connection not only between physical feelings and emotions, but also thoughts. Every heavily repeating thought, or a thought form, or a belief you entertain, will be reflected in a corresponding emotion and a body sensation or a body posture.

How do you feel about your emotions?

For example, if you routinely think of having to accomplish something to prove yourself worthy you might frequently feel the emotion of not being enough or of being empty within and you might even feel a fear of being alive. On the physical level, you may constantly slouch and feel a weight on your shoulders as if a heavy burden was actually present there, or you may feel "cold feet," or a certain emptiness or disconnection in your lower legs or ankles, almost as if your feet were not even touching the ground.

ONE MOON PRESENT formula takes all that into account and works with the interconnection of the mental, emotional, and physical levels, under the auspices of Spirit, the spiritual level.

In the example above, we may not be fully aware of our feelings of inadequacy or unworthiness, because they have perhaps been rendered subconscious. Consequently, we may live in denial of our exceeding ambition to succeed or of having to constantly compare and compete with others in order to soothe our wounded inner child and satisfy its need for recognition or praise. Many mind-created fears and problems may arise from such a condition.

The practice of ONE MOON PRESENT tools will help you become aware of where you are stuck, first on the physical level and then the emotional and mental mirror connections will become evident as well—when you are grounded and present enough and as the mind gradually releases its iron grip of control during regular breathwork meditations. Creative writing and self-love learning exercises will help you establish a new foundation for your balanced life, one full of joy and sweetness.

States of being

Some say that our emotions are located in the belly and thoughts in the head. I like to work with any coordinate system you might wish to use because we don't want to limit ourselves to the known and to what we're willing to believe. For argument's sake and for ease of explanation, let's follow the premise above.

So then, I ask you: what's in the heart?

If you say love, I agree. But what is love? Isn't love an emotion? Shouldn't it belong to the belly then?

No. You are right, because love is not an emotion. That's important. Love is a *state of being.* Just like peace and joy are. Again, we could use many coordinate systems and definitions, but deep inside, you know what I mean. There are levels of consciousness within that help us see love for what it truly is.

> Not all that you feel is a feeling.

A state of being is a consequence of awareness flowing through our being. The seat of awareness is in the heart. Our soul resides in our heart for as long as we're incarnated.

Now that's also the difference between true love (or unconditional love) and a conditional love which isn't even love at all. There are energies or aspects of energies acting upon us that we mistakenly perceive as love, but we're not going to talk about that here. For our work, it is enough to say that the feeling of butterflies in the belly isn't true love—and that's why infatuations come and go, especially when we're disappointed, hurt, or heart-broken— while true love is eternal and, yes, unconditional.

Another vital consequence of the distinction between states of being, like love, and emotions, is that while emotions are strongly mirrored in physical feelings and thoughts, love isn't and can independently co-exist with any or all emotions, feelings, and thoughts. Moreover, it mixes with them, it can embrace them and even transmute them to more love—not unlike fire and any material that can burn. Healing works because love is a state of being! We'll talk more about that in the next section.

During breathwork meditation, we patiently work with our energy and trust the breath to relax our mind so we can become more clearly aware of what is what—namely, of what love's true nature is: a manifestation of our soul dancing in our body. And while we open up to our stuck emotions and deal with our old hurts and physical discomforts, we still stay fully present with our love at all times. As we do that, we become aware of love and perceive it as a vibration which begins in the heart and then spreads throughout the body. We let it embrace all of our ailments, our imperfections and our problems, to make them go away—and love can really do that!

I firmly believe it is crucial for our self-healing method to work in a lasting and sustainable manner, that we do all our work ourselves, internally, by inviting the external agent—Spirit, Universe, God, Soul—to enter our sacred temple, the body. The responsibility and the power rest with us. It's all in our hands, and yet it isn't. It's a paradox that the mind is unable to unravel, and luckily, it never has to. It is enough to simply stay with the breath and remain conscious of everything we experience. Something larger than us—which is at the same time part of us—takes over and makes healing happen.

Mood

When I say mood, I'm not talking only about mood swings or moodiness. Simply put, mood is how we feel about our day, and also how we feel about our feelings, emotions, thoughts, ourselves, our lives and the world in general. It's a complex conglomerate of subtle, all-inclusive, omni-directional perception, both externally and internally oriented. It's where our feelings, emotions, and thoughts come together with our awareness.

For our healing process, it's vital we warm up to the idea that our mood is something that we may be able to choose, or intend—at least on some levels. It's not just an arbitrary emotional state that we get thrown into by circumstances. Mood is our response to the circumstances, and it is where our character shows—and depending on the clarity of our consciousness, we can avoid many pitfalls of prejudice, convictions, beliefs, and other programming, when we choose our responses to life's situations.

Another way of talking about mood is to liken it to weather. Of course, mood swings have been compared to weather before, nothing new here. The point I'm illustrating with this example is how the element of choice comes into the game—something we'll go deeper into in the next section. The feelings, emotions, and thoughts themselves may be more or less outside of our control, like most circumstances generally are. And our mood on a certain level may still not be something we can create or direct at will. But our perception of, and our response to our mood is already one level closer to the place of our command or choice.

You are layered like a dream within a dream.

Back to weather. When it rains, we can't stop that. What we can do is make a choice: either we try to stay dry or we could choose to dance and sing in the rain. But even if we choose the former, we might still get wet involuntarily—it was obviously outside of our control. *Now* what we *can* choose is our response to what happened to us: we can get upset or just unhappy, or we can choose not to linger on it for long and instead change our clothes and get on with our day.

Going deeper, perhaps rainy weather makes us sad and such a response is beyond our choice—because of our subconscious programming. Or we may be trying hard to like the cold weather, but keep failing at it. And then we get disappointed by our failure to stay positive in that regard. So many levels there!

If we look at our feelings, emotions, and thoughts instead of the weather phenomena now, we may observe we have a similar response to them: our mood is our response. And then we have a response to our mood, which is mood again, but on another level. For example, if we get angry with our child for getting wet in the rain we may feel guilty because of our perhaps unwarranted or exaggerated anger. We may feel inadequate as a parent or even a failure as a human being, if we are inclined or programmed that way. In turn, our mood would probably shift to heavy and unpleasant. And if that is something that we experience often, we may have already anticipated it happening and feared it, or we may feel a leaden weight of being stuck in a vicious circle with seemingly no way out.

Thus, we've come a long way from an innocent accident of getting wet in the rain, through many levels of responses to a response (i.e. many levels of moods), and ultimately to a somber mood of "everything is wrong in the world" in a matter of seconds. The more we struggle to stay afloat, the more we sink into the quicksand of—trickery of the programming!

Before we discuss a way out of this nightmare, in the next section, one last definition. *Prevalent mood* is the general feeling about our life that we've settled upon: the way we see ourselves and our role in the world. For the example above, the prevalent mood could be depression. And the way we create and reinforce our prevalent mood to ourselves by the internal dialog we incessantly repeat in the mind, is what I call "our old story."

So how do we get out of there? The way out is through.

Summary

What did we learn in this section?

Feelings and emotions are not the same thing, even though they mirror each other, and they mirror thoughts as well. Love isn't an emotion but a state of being. It comes with awareness and coexists with emotions and uplifts them. Mood is our current, inner response to all of the above. There are countless levels of mood as we keep responding to our own responses. Prevalent mood is our overall response to ourselves and life in general. In the next section, we'll consider whether we are free to choose our prevalent mood unconditionally.

What is healing?

I've been stuck at writing this section for some time. There is no linear way to express what healing truly is. If there was, we wouldn't need healing and books like this.

It's circular. Whatever I could write, there would always be something left out or described incompletely. Why? Well, that's exactly the core of what I'm trying to address. See, it's circular.

The good news is that it doesn't matter in the least!

> Just reading this now is already healing!

Indeed, for our healing, we don't have to understand how it works. What we need to understand and believe is: that we are stuck, that we need healing, and that there is a way (many ways actually) of getting there.

If you don't believe that you are stuck and need healing, then this book is for you. It can help you open up to that idea and make a choice to accept it. Of course, the best way to do that is to play along and do some of the work—and experience healing first-hand.

And that's the gist of what I decided to put in this section. I merely want you to pause and seriously consider giving this book a proper chance. Perhaps thirty more minutes of your time. You don't have much to lose, but maybe you can gain something indescribable! I'm not talking about awakening or enlightenment here—but I'm not negating it either…

If you do believe you are stuck and if you can feel it, even daily perhaps, read on and we'll delineate a practical formula for approaching that in the next chapter.

Before we go there, let me still try to verbalize what I believe healing is. In a most simple way, it's a process of improving the quality of your life. Whatever you want and expect from life, healing can make it easier and faster to get there. If you're confused and don't know what you want, healing can help you find out. And lastly, if you're in any way split within and a part of you resists what you want, healing can put all that into another, clearer perspective and lead you to an empowered state where you will be able to make your best choice.

Sounds just too good to be true? Well, that's because it's circular.

If you're willing to learn more about healing, the following subsections will provide the gist of the theory behind its workings. Or, as I keep saying, you can jump ahead and give a try to the breathwork meditation or another tool from the ONE MOON PRESENT toolbox.

Spirit moving

I can't put it more bluntly than this:

> Spirit moving is the only thing that matters.

But what does that even mean? When we wish to understand the infinite universe with a linear mind, it can mean many things.

To express it a bit poetically: to be alive before we die! Without consciousness, who are we? A slab of meat going through the motions on an auto-pilot? An emotional punching bag or a bomb waiting to explode? Can we appreciate anything without feeling it first? If we are not present in awareness, do we exist at all? How real are we? How real is our life? Where our attention goes, energy flows. There is always something more.

Instead of asking you the trick question "who are you?", I ask you: What do you want? What do you want to express in this life?

What is your so-called mission, or purpose in life? If you don't know that, can you make it up—right now? Yes, you *can* do that!

If you can open up to imagine the whole of your being in this lifetime, with all the possibilities and potential, all the choices and paths that lie behind you and also stretch before you—what do you feel? Are you scared? Many of us are too afraid to grab the wheel of our own destiny. We fear we may break something or do something wrong. But that's not how it works. It is not only our birthright, but actually our sacred duty to assume complete responsibility for who we are here and now, in this marvelous world!

Once you feel that kind of freedom that comes from such awakened consciousness, everything is possible. For every obstacle or challenge you will find a way or a tool. An abundance of energy and all other resources will be granted to you directly by the Universe so you can accomplish whatever mission you choose to embark on as an adventure of fun, joy, and love.

From what I see, we need two things to make that happen. We have to ground our visions into the reality of our life and we must allow Spirit to keep moving through us.

Without the former, we are merely daydreamers who will die with either a faint smile on our lips or a deep frown on our brow for not having realized our dreams. Without the latter, we are overzealous, ambitious bullies who will force and destroy whatever it takes to have it our way, never reaching a closure or satisfaction with anything we do.

Without the grounding in Mother Earth and without Father Spirit supporting us from within, we are ultimately alone, all by ourselves, separated from everything and everyone else, disconnected, until we eventually wilt and die. We are a phantom living among ghosts in a world of shadows.

But if we can change one iota of that, if we can experience Spirit moving in our body while being rooted firmly in Nature, everything starts to make sense. It's never too late for that. ONE MOON PRESENT formula is designed to get us there.

Free will and the element of choice

The million-dollar, age-old question of whether we possess free will (and what is free will anyway?) is closely tied to the ancient saying *know thyself* and the question of "who are you?" To me, again, both are trick questions that have no single, one-dimensional answers. Let's focus merely on how it pertains to our process of healing.

Surely you notice how dualistic you can be, "in your mind," as they say? One part of you wants to eat cake, and another wants to lose weight or simply live healthy. Which part should you listen to? Which part is right? Can it be that both are? Great questions.

We could list countless examples like the one above from our daily lives. Let's save us the time and jump straight to the point. I believe we live in a world of multiple truths. There just is no single ultimate, absolute and objective truth. I'm not talking about the origins of the universe or the fundamental laws of physics and metaphysics here. I'm saying that for practically every nuance in everyday life, many viewpoints may hold true simultaneously.

Should I stay, or should I go? Fight or flight? Left or right? Embrace or set boundaries? Speak my mind and potentially hurt somebody or suppress my own feelings and hurt myself? Ask for little and remain humble or dream big and manifest abundance?

So many questions! What to choose? What is the *right* choice for *you*?

It's impossible to tell. Nobody knows. There is no authority on that, not even God or Spirit. There is nobody who would know that, for *you*—other than you! At least a part of you knows, always, even though you may never understand it fully. But, wait! We're back at square one then. *Which* part knows? Which part is right?

> Thou art god!

What I choose to believe is: it doesn't matter. Pick any part you like and trust it. Follow its advice about what step to take next, if you want. *That* is your choice. That's your free will. You decide what is right for you by *creating* your truth within!

In practice, you find (or pave) a way to get clear about what is what in your life. What do you really want, long-term and right now? How do you get there? What do you need to do, or stop doing? What is preventing you, blocking you?

Healing can help you along the way with getting to the clarity and releasing the blocks of your stuck emotions and beliefs.

Let's try another simple practical experiment. On the level of awareness, draw an abstract line to summarize how you feel in this certain moment: the total of your sentiments, beliefs, circumstances—all of it at once, in one flash of our perceived mood. And then, just ask yourself point blank: how do you feel about *that*—how do you feel about your mood? And once again, when you receive the answer, whatever it is, you *still* have a choice to repeat the question, as many times as you wish, because there is always more—always another level.

The true element of choice is our response to our other responses, even the ones we can't control—or so we may believe. You see, that's the key shift right there: on top of layers upon layers of subconscious strata of programming and inherited patterns and many layers of our responses and interpretations there is always another extra layer that belongs to our free-will choice! No matter how stuck we may feel, no matter how much we may be suffering, no matter how confused and powerless we are—at any given moment we can just cut through all of that in one swift move and *create our choice*, which can be anything at all.

Nothing and nobody can ever take that level of choice away from us. The main element of healing is to learn that and put it to moment-to-moment practice. Sometimes the key lies just in remembering that we have the free-will choice of response, at the crucial moment.

Creating self-love

If everything is so circular how can we ever break free?

What I love about this healing modality I practice and teach, is that it makes for a pleasant and joyful journey. Yes, there is discipline and work involved, and facing the heavy feelings at times—but always from the safety and comfort of our own free-will choice and self-love.

Self-love makes every zone the comfort zone, so we never have to leave it in order to facilitate learning or healing. We employ the fact that love is a state of being and can co-exist with any emotion. Healing happens when we are patient enough and willing to experience our shadow side—the negative feelings, emotions, and thoughts—together with our light-creating side, our soul's self-love vibration.

In every situation, we have a choice. When we get triggered by a hurtful word, by a scary thought, or simply by any unwanted feelings, we can decide to face that and deal with it immediately—using our healing methods—or choose to save it for a later time. It's a valid, free-will choice, as always.

Through time and practice, we develop our awareness to be able to respond consciously instead of reacting subconsciously. By the time we get to the point when we can make a clear choice whether to deal with a trigger now or leave it for later, we can say we're already pretty much healed.

At that stage, we enter a certain presence that we never completely lose again. We remain aware at almost all times that the feelings, emotions, and thoughts we have aren't something we ever need to control, improve, or fix in any way. The element of choice doesn't even have to pertain to them directly—we merely choose and keep choosing our responses and how we respond to our responses.

In a way, we don't need the wisdom to distinguish between what we can and what we can't change in our lives. That knowing would soon become circular again. I find it much clearer and more direct to focus on where I want to go in the first place and simply deal with the resistance and obstacles as I encounter them, in a loving and creative way.

> To love is to create.

That's why creativity is of utmost importance in the process of healing. It always works—albeit in mysterious ways—and we don't need to understand a thing to employ it at any given moment. As opposed to the mind, which is constantly toiling to control everything in life, our intuition- and soul-based creativity is pure freedom! We create our responses to internal and external circumstances, we create our very truth and reality, we even create our *self-love* as a complete, all-inclusive state of being.

I love my mind, as I love my emotions and feelings. I aspire to bring balance into my life which would equally include these three sides, together with the spiritual side. There is no fullness to my experience otherwise.

To get there, I'm constantly learning new aspects of self-love. I use creativity in my healing process to keep developing my awareness and intuition. I'm out-creating my old story by loving my shadows in a grounded way. That's what ONE MOON PRESENT formula is all about, as we'll soon find out.

Summary

Healing is a pragmatic way to improve the quality of your life. In order to break the seemingly endless, vicious circle of our programming and past traumas, we learn to choose our responses and out-create the old story where we are stuck. Self-love and creativity are the master keys to healing.

Let's see what ONE MOON PRESENT healing formula is and how it can indeed change your life!

III. ONE MOON PRESENT:
Your shiny new toolbox

Do we really have to *do* the work?

Yes, and it is a pleasure, joyful and fun!

I promised you less-to-zero theory in these last chapters, so I'll go straight to the pragmatic point.

Your whole life you've been repeating certain patterns of behavior and programs of perception. There's lots of inertia in that. If what you kept repeating brought you to a point where you feel stuck and perhaps even afraid, well, perhaps it's time to shift the patterns and deprogram your life.

This work is nothing more than a way of doing things in your life differently. It's an adventure, something fresh and exciting. It's a new hope, and at the same time, your old dream finally coming true.

Carefully observing what works and what doesn't in my own process of healing and with others I've been honored to work with, I've devised ONE MOON PRESENT formula in a simple yet potent manner that addresses all the key elements a global shift in life needs.

Before I describe the formula and its five elements, let me summarize the rationale behind it in a paragraph. Why does this method of healing work?

The trick is to stay with it until you get momentum. As you focus your attention on the healing exercises and meditation, your daily life energy is redirected there instead of being wasted on old, self-destructive patterns of behavior. The more energy you reroute to your healing, the stronger and the sooner it happens. The exercises help you focus on the flow, and the meditation helps you defocus from the obstructions.

One Moon Present

What's in a name?

If you're a practical person you'll love this part of the book. Apart from the poetic and somewhat abstract title of this section, which is also the name of the whole toolbox I'm offering to you, this chapter is as plain and clear as a sunny day. First, allow me to explain the *One Moon Present*.

In a blast of intuition, I knew this powerful and trusty toolbox must have a name of its own. Instantly, this poetic name came to me—before I even grasped the dual nature of its meaning.

The tools, the breathwork meditation, and the creative writing and self-love exercises all follow a simple time-frame formula that goes on for nearly a whole calendar month and then repeats from the beginning on the next arm of the "spiritual spiral". As *staying present* is one of the tools in this formula, I feel that the sound of "one moon present" has a similar ring to "one year sober". When you've stayed present for a whole moon cycle—congratulations! And that's what we'll accomplish.

The other meaning is an homage to our dear Mother Earth without whom none of this would be possible. The Moon has a powerful presence in my own life, as it does in everybody's, I believe. Our healing work will begin with a new moon to make plans and set intentions, then proceed towards the full moon when clarity and light will come to us. Then, we'll complete the cycle by grounding the lessons into the waning moon. All in all, it will be a veritable present we give to ourselves as if a gift from the moon: one moon present!

Enough of poetry, now down to the business of healing.

The not so secret formula

Remember that you're here of your own accord. In this life, in this moment, reading this line and choosing your healing. In the same vein it's entirely up to you whether you will commit to doing the ONE MOON PRESENT work for the duration of a whole moon cycle.

If the timing is off and the new moon is weeks away, no matter. If you don't feel like hesitating you can still start today and it will work out just fine. The mind will be patient and it will trust and adapt. Where there's a will, there's a way. So make it happen if you care to.

There are five ingredients to the formula I propose you do daily for the maximum effect. Try it and see if it brings you the results you desire. What do you have to lose?

In the subsequent sections, I'll describe the five tools one by one. There are no rules about how you execute them. Find your own way. Listen to your body, emotions, mind, and Spirit—and trust your intuition to lead you.

However, *all* of the five elements should be engaged and *exchanged* with daily, or almost daily, for reasons our minds are at first unable to understand. Working together in harmonic agreement, like five fingers of the hand, they will cover all the bases and avoid the blind spots that could slow us down or even block our progress entirely.

> The healing work and ONE MOON PRESENT formula work best if practiced daily.

Please, bear with me and ask yourself again if you're willing to trust the work enough to just do it and experience what it does first hand. You don't need to understand more of it than you already do.

You don't need perfection or a better opportunity: you're ready, or you wouldn't be reading this now!

Read carefully about *grounding, staying present, meditating, writing creatively,* and *learning self-love.* Make notes—organize yourself at your own pace and leisure, and prepare your own plan, your personal recipe for healing.

If you prefer the clear structure of a solid time-table, write it down, put it into your computer or smartphone, and set the necessary alarms and reminders. Get willing, get ready, then let go and just do it, do the work daily. Let it become your new routine, one that you can already sense will introduce a major difference in life.

Now, this is where you come in and take over!

Cheat Sheet: One Moon Present

START

↓

Tool #1 — Grounding
Tool #2 — Staying Present
Tool #3 — Breathwork Meditation
Tool #4 — Creative Writing
Tool #5 — Learning Self-Love

↓

 Repeat daily for 28 days

↓

SELF-LOVE HEALING

Grounding

Grounding is the simplest and most elementary of all the tools of ONE MOON PRESENT. It's also the most crucial at the beginning of your road to healing.

It works best—it works miracles, in fact—without any prior experience or knowledge, and without training. You don't have to understand anything. You don't even have to do any work.

Now that we've come this far and your heart is ready to generate some trust, you can approach this humble tool with the solemn attention it deserves. I invite you—perhaps more than with any of the other four tools—to treat grounding as a sacred ancient ritual, no less.

Every day, at a time you may choose and schedule in advance, make a conscious commitment to use the entirety of one single minute solely for yourself. It can be more than one minute if you wish, but don't go overboard. Sometimes, less *is* more.

How *do* you ground?

First, set your phone to silent. (Your mind as well.) Leave it on the nightstand and forget about technology and social engagement for a moment. Instead, focus within, specifically on your body and bodily feelings.

Stand up. How does that feel? What do you feel in your legs?

If you have an opportunity, step outside and walk a few paces on earth, soil, grass, or pavement—it's all Earth. It's all Ground and it grounds us if we submit to it and love it.

Even if you're in the city and maybe on the sixtieth floor, that's not a problem. Mother Earth encompasses all of existence. To Her, nothing is unnatural or artificial. Ultimately, everything is created and constructed of organic, natural materials. We're all made of stardust!

Stand still on the spot that invites you. Wherever you feel safe, relaxed, happy. Home.

Now gently close your eyes. You can smile an inner smile.

Our sense of vision is predominant, so that's why we close our eyes—to be able to focus better on the other four senses.

What do you hear? Listen to all the sounds, pleasant or not. Remember, you're grounding to the reality of *what is*. Whatever is in your surroundings, simply perceive it, listen to it. You don't have to judge or analyze it in any way. Just notice the sounds you hear.

Now focus on the smell and the scents around you. Perhaps you can smell roses, or foul odors—it's all the same, for grounding. Just notice it. Take it in, then release it out again. Let it flow through you. We're learning not to control the flow. Perhaps you can smell something neutral and subtle, like the air after rain. You can smell Spring.

What do you feel on your skin? Is there wind? Sunshine? Do you feel slightly hot or mildly cold? Are you freezing, perhaps? It's all good! Just feel it, but do take complete care of your body. This exercise is not one of drastic measures.

Maybe you can even taste something? Some eastern spiritual schools talk about a connection between our sense of taste and a shift in consciousness. For example, you may discover a faint metallic taste in your mouth as your attention flows to your spiritual and energetic side.

Now *connect* to Mother Earth! This is what grounding truly means. Feel Mother Nature, smell her, taste her, sense her, intuit her deepest and sweetest essence. Love her. Touch her heart!

If you want you can now open your eyes and look around, take in everything as if you are seeing it for the first time in your life. Cliche or not, feel and trust that love is in the air.

Make grounding a sacred ritual

Never forget, grounding is a feeling. At a certain point, it becomes a state of being. It makes no sense to use the *grounding* tool without that awareness. Merely going through the motions will not bring about the healing you seek to create. The true engagement lies in the attention to your feelings. It is a sacred process.

I want to be as clear as possible here, because this is of utmost importance and all the other tools work in conjunction with *grounding*. It is not enough to merely pause your day for a minute, or run away from your life as we often do, even using meditation as an excuse. The key to grounding lies in the connection to everything, within and without, below and above, left and right, right and wrong, good and bad.

Connect to Mother Earth and let go completely.

So when you stand out there on your lawn, or in the center of your living room, stop controlling the process and trying to affect the outcome. Instead, focus exclusively on your perception and your senses, both internally and externally. Observe what is flowing all around and through you. Feel that flow and sense that you *are* an inseparable part of it. You *are* that flow, together with everything else in existence. Let that realization make you happy and fulfilled with gratitude and affection for all there is. That's the sensation of oneness.

When you lose yourself in the scents of freshly mowed grass or the coolness of the morning breeze, and when that carries you back in time to memories of your childhood so you shudder and smile—that's when you're *grounding*!

You haven't just escaped to daydreaming. This is something else. You've transcended the programs of perception and become timeless. You're singularly present with the total awareness of your reality and your whole life at once. Nothing else matters at that moment. You have arrived.

Cheat Sheet: Grounding

START

↓

#1 — Silence your phone (and mind)

#2 — Stand up and feel your body

#3 — Close your eyes and smile

#4 — Listen, smell, feel, taste

#5 — Connect to Mother Earth

#6 — Let go of all control

#7 — Be aware of the Flow of Oneness

↓

GROUNDING

Staying present

Look around you. What do you see? What attracts your attention?

The shape of a flower reaching upwards, a pair of pink and orange lamps by the TV, a wooden pencil on your desk?

Whatever it is, can you feel it, sense it, intuit it? Can you connect to it deeply, even to the point of loving it?

Now close your eyes and draw a deep breath. Let go. Don't try to do anything specific. Simply be.

Open your eyes again and look around once more. Can you feel the special quality of being present?

This is it!

You are alive, right here and now. You are you. Your life is unfolding in this very moment, and with absolute certainty you know that one fine day, this very life will end and you'll die.

Regarding all the emotions about that notion, you do not hide or run away. Use the sensation of impermanence as a fuel for consciousness! Evanescence is such a beautiful word. Feel its full depth. Like the moon is waning and waxing, so are our lives.

Is there trust in your heart that there is life after death? Your soul is singing a song about your immortality. Like the sun is a constant and eternal presence, so is your soul.

Simply looking around you, examining life and the elements of life, is a part of staying present. Taking it all in, the good, the not so good, and the undecided as well.

Let's lean towards the undecided. The unspecified. Neither good nor bad. Neutral. Unlabeled, untouched by the mind. Uncategorized by the mind.

Take your time to feel.

Go out there and live fully. Experience the contrast between the inner and the outer, between the temporary and the eternal. Our potential for consciousness grows by exercising awakening.

However, our attention span is limited by the available energy we have. Sooner or later, everything runs out, even the consciousness. It will invariably happen every time after you have an awakening experience. But there is no need to fear the ebb of consciousness, because we can and will awaken again, and again, and again.

Staying present is meditation

While *grounding* is geared toward honing your awareness, *staying present* is meant to enhance your consciousness. In plain words, we ground to feel alive and we stay present to feel who we are, to know ourselves.

Like with grounding, there are no rules about using this tool. Remember that the mind can't help us here. The goal is to ease into a state of trust where we no longer rely on the mind to figure out everything and tell us what to do. That in itself is liberating.

Anything that can make you feel more connected to the *above*, to the skies and stars, to Spirit, can be used as a way to enhance consciousness. And without consciousness, there can be no healing.

One way to silence the mind quickly, is to stop breathing altogether. If we remain completely motionless, as if frozen from within, the mind pauses, because there is nothing left for it to control. But we can't keep our breath forever. As soon as we breathe in again, the mind gets agitated with a renewed zest and explodes in frantic activity.

I used to meditate like that. I struggled to silence the thoughts. I fought to control my mind. I didn't realize that I was the mind, trying to control, well, everything.

Some say the way out is in. Or through.

Learning—by experiencing it through breathwork meditation—about the essential difference between mind/thoughts and awareness/consciousness helped me trust Spirit and abandon myself to it completely. There is no need to control anything. What freedom comes with that feeling!

Nowadays, my meditation is different. I could say that life itself is my meditation. Being here, fully present with all my feelings, emotions, and even thoughts. Not yearning to become something else, or more. Not craving or clinging to anything.

We could say that staying present is the practice of constantly re-awakening to who you truly are. Who are you? Keep asking the question without looking for a definitive answer.

Awaken to your innermost choice.

While you can do the *grounding* exercise once a day at a certain time, *staying present* may appear to be more about continuity throughout the whole day. In that respect, the two seem almost the opposites to each other.

But that is not entirely so. In fact, the two tools work together so seamlessly that it's often impossible to tell them apart. Through dedicated practice, we learn to keep grounding many times a day without even trying.

The song of a bird or a ray of sunshine simply yanks our attention away from our everyday business. Or it can be something less pleasant yet equally real—like a traffic jam—that inspires our grounding.

The same goes for our practice of staying present. A troubling thought or a harsh emotion may invite us to a tiny awakening, or a little enlightenment, as I like to look at it. We will have developed our consciousness enough to stay aware and remember that it is always our choice how we respond.

Soon, instead of succumbing to each and every daily problem that presents to us and losing our time, energy, and clarity to it—we will use that same negativity as fuel for more consciousness and self-love! For me, that's the true meaning of "what doesn't kill you, makes you stronger". The trick is in staying sober enough to catch ourselves from falling into the fog of old programming. The trick is in—staying present.

Another way of describing this tool in comparison to grounding is to say that while grounding is about consciously perceiving and observing the external, staying present starts from the inside out. In the end, the two practices meet and intertwine—in the reality of our life.

It is best to keep returning to the practice of staying present—which is actually just a moment of remembering, and then another moment, and another—as many times a day as we can. In time, the frequency, the quantity, and the quality of our momentary awakenings will increase naturally. Awareness can be trained like a muscle until we get fit, as fit as we want to be.

Staying present exercises

Let me delineate two basic exercises to help us with this training of consciousness. They are not my inventions. I learned the former from Carlos Castaneda's books (which helped me immensely and still inspire me) and the latter from James Mahu and his Wingmakers materials (to whom I feel closely connected as well).

This exercise is almost too plain to call it an exercise, but it's incredibly effective if we practice it consistently and with dedication. Every time you put on your shoes or socks, or remove them, make sure you do the left foot first and then the right. You'll see how often you'll find yourself forgetting all about it and performing this mundane task routinely, as we normally do.

The key lies in developing awareness. As soon as you get used to putting your left shoe first and it becomes a routine for you—there is no sense in practicing it any longer. At that point you should change the rules. For example, switch from *left first* to *right first*. And by all means, feel free to modify and apply this exercise to anything in your daily life. Everything that you do routinely can be used as a training ground for your awareness through this technique.

Intend to remain awake.

The other exercise is called *quantum breath*. It is similarly simple but again extremely potent. I recommend setting a timer or alarm several times a day and without hesitation, jumping to perform the exercise when it goes off, pausing anything you might be caught doing. The harder it is for you to let go and switch to doing the quantum breath, the better results it will yield.

You should perform four breaths one after another in the following manner. You can breathe through the mouth or the nose, as you wish. First, inhale a slow, deep breath for the count of four—the unit could be seconds, or not, it doesn't matter—and you can go faster or slower, again, as you decide. Second, hold the breath in for the same count of four. Third, gradually release the breath out, while counting to four the same way. And lastly, hold your breath out, again for the same count. You just did four stages of equal duration: inhalation, pause, exhalation, pause.

That was one quantum breath. Repeat it three more times: four in total. It will take you roughly a minute to complete the whole exercise.

Be patient with yourself as you learn. After you get some experience with it, you can embellish the inhaling phase by visualizing, imagining, or sensing how your soul, or Spirit, is entering your body. While you keep the breath within, you can feel "complete, fully present, truly You". During the exhalation, you can imagine releasing everything temporary and ephemeral from your body and connecting directly to the Source or to all there is. And when you hold your breath in the last stage, you can be aware of "being One with All".

I have been performing quantum breath daily, four or five times a day, for several years now. It helps me both ground and stay present every time I honestly dedicate myself to doing it, by applying myself fully. Even the choice of letting go of whatever important project I am working on for a minute to engage in something so abstract and spiritual makes all the difference. And then the magic of breath and the flow of feelings do the rest.

Cheat Sheet: Staying Present

START

#1 — Pause and look around you

#2 — Take your time and feel inside

#3 — Remember you have a choice

#4 — Ask yourself who you are

#5 — Feel alive

#6 — Feel happy and grateful to be alive

#7 — Intend to stay awake

STAYING PRESENT

Cheat Sheet: Quantum Breath

START

↓

#1 — Inhale slowly for the count of four
#2 — Hold your breath for the count of four
#3 — Exhale slowly for the count of four
#4 — Pause for the count of four

↓

 Repeat four times in total

↓

QUANTUM BREATH

Breathwork meditation

I firmly believe this tool is central to healing and key to everybody's well-being in life.

When I first encountered my friend David Elliott and his healing method—of which the breathwork meditation is the centerpiece—my life was in shreds and I was ready to give up without even realizing it. Practicing this powerful, gentle, and active meditation daily—sometimes even twice in a row—restored my energy and my hope, my trust in love and in being able to *live a balanced life full of sweetness* once again—words David prescribed to me as a healing mantra.

After more than eight years of staying present and exchanging with the meditation, I can safely say that it saved my life and my soul. Yes, I know: a bold statement, but one that I can testify to and show up for.

Even if you don't feel confident about using the other four tools, breathwork meditation alone will lead you, gradually and steadily, through the hardest days into more consciousness and self-love—simply by practicing it.

How is breathwork meditation done?

Simply put, you lie down and breathe consciously through the mouth in a two-stage pattern while listening to a guiding voice and relaxing music. Near the end you start to breathe normally again, relax, and recharge. Keep your attention focused on your body and feelings, and let your emotions flow freely when they arise.

There is an abundance of detail that I could tell you here. But this tool is all about practice, so I will keep this section as short as I can. If you are weary of theory and eager to do the work, feel free to skip or skim this section—and just try the meditation. You can always return for more information when you get genuinely interested. However, I want to stress two points right from the start.

Committing to the breath

Firstly, the breathwork meditation will work only when you actually do it, and the more regularly you do it, the better. So if you are truly serious about your healing, book your time for this. It doesn't have to be long. David claims that 7 minutes a day is enough and I tend to agree.

I prepared and included a 14-minute meditation recording for you that you can freely access at this link:

freemeditation14.onemoonpresent.com.

I invite you to start working with it. If harsh emotions are what you wish to address, this recording has a built-in intention for that subject. Nevertheless, my experience has been that when we surrender to the guidance of Spirit, the subjects and the objects don't matter that much. Any breathwork meditation will bring about results, when you do it.

What do I mean by that? Well, there are other recordings out there. At the time of writing this, I'm getting ready to release nine of them myself. There are over twenty of David Elliott's powerful recordings available, and I'm sure you can find a plethora of others on your own.

When you feel you are ready to go deeper with One Moon Present formula, I recommend you start working with its full-length, 28-minute meditation, or with any of the *Love Yourself Through* meditations, which focus specifically on fear, anger, or sadness. You can find them on my website **onemoonpresent.com**. (See the back of this book for more information).

Meditate as much as you can, even when it gets gritty.

Whatever breathwork meditation you use, the important part is that you approach it diligently and respectfully. If you can't find the time or the energy to meditate every day, a few times a week is also great.

It's better not to obsess about doing it *every* day without exception. We're human beings living in a real world and anything can happen. Let's trust we'll find the time and be grateful for each occasion we're able to meditate.

Exchanging with the breath

The second point I want to make is about the quality of the practice. Like with everything else in our lives, there is not much sense in doing it just for outward appearances, just so we can tick a checkbox and be done with it. That's a waste of time and a waste of our precious hope and intent, because we dilute it with our disrespect.

Therefore, besides our dedication to the *quantity*—or the frequency of a regular and steady practice—I invite you to consider committing yourself to its *quality* as well.

> Treat breathwork as sacred.

Treat each time you practice breathwork meditation as a sacred ritual. Plan your time accordingly. Make sure nobody will disturb you. Prepare yourself a safe space where you can feel cozy and comfortable. Use essential oils if you have them and burn some sage, cedar, or palo santo wood, or perhaps light a tea candle during your practice to support your intent.

What I find of utmost importance is that we intend to consciously *exchange* with the meditation. What does that mean? It means we not only expect to receive a gift of healing from Spirit, but we are also willing to give something in return. Something worthy: our time, our attention, our presence, our awareness.

Exchange, as defined by my friend David, is not a simple quid-pro-quo though. We will not be measuring and comparing the two sides of the scales to see if we paid enough to get what we want. That's the merchant way of the mind and the love of power.

Instead, we will exchange by way of *loving*! We will cherish each and every breath we take. We will ground in our body and feelings, emotions, and thoughts. We will stay present with our whole and total experience while we meditate. We will consciously release our control in the mind and abandon ourselves to the trust in our heart.

We will melt into the moment and into a reality larger than life.

You'll see. When this is only theory with lots of big words, it doesn't do justice to the juice of experiencing it first-hand. But as soon as you will start to breathe, you'll know what I mean without a shadow of doubt.

Preparing for the meditation

The meditation is done lying down on your back, either on the floor using a yoga mat, on a massage table, or simply in your bed or on the sofa. Even outside on the grass is perfect, too.

Relax comfortably. There is no need to strain any part of your body or exert yourself in any way. The maximum effect will be achieved when you soften within and stop taking yourself and your healing process too seriously.

Why so serious? Smile.

It's best not to prop your head too much. If you do need a support for your neck, that's fine, but try to keep your air passages unobstructed so your breath and energy can flow clearly.

We'll breathe with our eyes closed. If you have a yoga eye pillow, it can assist you at calming your mind right from the start. I love the scent of lavender which is often used in those eye pillows.

Setting the intent

Just before you start with the active breathing, it's the time to set your intention, or *intent*.

Setting your intent is as easy as choosing what you want to create in your life. Here are some examples: *I want less stress. I intend my physical healing. I will write a book. I'd like to create a better relationship with my wife.*

Be specific. The more specific you get, the better. If you already know more about yourself and where you may be stuck, you can set a detailed intent. For example: *I want to address my fear of speaking in public; I want to get clear about my feelings of unworthiness and my belief that I have nothing of value to say; I intend to create more confidence and self-love around that.* That is all one single intent.

How is intending different from merely wishing something?

In the shamanic tradition revealed by Carlos Castaneda's teacher don Juan, intent is seen as an impersonal, universal force of infinite magnitude and mysterious nature which can never be understood by the mind alone. It belongs to the category of the *unknowable.*

For all practical purposes and, well, intents, we can safely say that intent is Spirit, or Universe, or Mother Nature, or even God, if you wish. In any case, we're talking about a profound feeling, a special sense, and *beckoning intent* during the meditation is a purely spiritual and abstract endeavor. Nobody understands how it is done and how it works, yet we can do it and pragmatically attest to its results in the world of everyday life.

When I lead a live meditation, right before we enter the active phase, I invite everybody to place their hands palm-down onto their chests over the heart and deeply feel within. You can do that too at this point during your meditation practice.

Ask your whole being: what is it that I want? What do I wish for more than anything else? What is my heart's and soul's true desire? What do I want to experience or express in my life? What is my mission, my life's purpose? What do I want to create and manifest, today and for the rest of my days? Also, what is it that I *don't* want? Where do I feel stuck? What do I want to change in my life? What do I want to address and heal today?

The more you circumvent the thought-controlled processes and directly feel your burning questions as long-unanswered emotions or never-addressed feelings, the more in touch you will get with intent, or Spirit—and the greater your chances of manifesting your new choices.

Let the answers come to you, effortlessly, with no obsessions. Don't chase them or cling to any old, mental-based cravings. Open up to your soul and Spirit and allow the insights and visions to flow into your attention.

Even if nothing comes up or you feel confused and don't understand the process, you can just make the answers up! No, I'm not kidding. The intent is closely tied to intuition and intuition works hand in hand with imagination—the three I's of the soul. Choose to trust the process and enjoy the ride. Make it up: what is it that you want the most in your life right now? It should be easy.

Now that you have all the questions and answers ready, combine all that you stirred up into a singular vision that you want to realize: a moment in your future when it has already happened. Your vision doesn't have to be purely visual—perhaps sounds, smells, and other perceptions came to you in a flash of intuition. Feel as if you are there, living it.

> Set your intent and feel it already manifesting.

Take spiritual note of your vision and *set the intent to manifest it*—without needing to understand how. Believe you can do that, then do it and believe you've done it. It's a matter of faith and trust in your own secret, sacred capabilities as a human being.

Proceed with the breathwork. When the time is right, the intent will ignite of itself and the manifestation will occur.

The two-stage breathing pattern

The core element of this breathwork method is the two-stage pattern of breathing. In the first phase of the meditation, which is called the active phase, you will breathe consistently through the mouth in the following manner: two inhalations, one exhalation. Open up your air passages and let the energy flow freely.

> Two breaths in. One breath out. Through the mouth.

Effectively, split the inhalation into two halves. Draw the first breath into the lower abdomen, energetically speaking, preferably all the way down to the second chakra around the sexual organs, where our emotions are often trapped. Take the second breath high into the upper chest, while lifting the energy up through the heart where it can get transmuted by our self-love. The exhalation can be natural, or only slightly accelerated, but still done through the mouth.

> Breath one: lower abdomen. Breath two: upper chest.

There will be a person breathing with you in the background of the recording, but you don't have to match their speed or intensity. You can go slower, faster, softer, or deeper. Listen to your body and energy and find your own rhythm. There is no wrong way of doing the breathwork meditation.

Nevertheless, this is not about hyperventilating, so keep it easy and steady. We want to build our energy gradually through time to create a profound and lasting effect.

Focus on your feelings.

Some time into the breathwork, the energies will start moving and emotions will hopefully flow. That can cause us to feel colder or warmer than expected. I find it prudent to have a blanket ready just in case, even if the space is warm when you begin. Wear loose, comfortable clothing.

It's important we keep well hydrated when doing any kind of spiritual practice and breathwork is no exception. Drink clear water before you start. If you drank too much, it's okay to go to the bathroom even in the middle of meditation.

The resistance

This is a good place to mention the *resistance* that will invariably enter your practice. This method is free of rules, so everything goes: we'll be releasing our emotions, perhaps sobbing, crying, shouting, yelling, and maybe even slapping the ground with our hands in conscious outbursts.

Trust the breathwork meditation the way we perform it. Thousands upon thousands of practitioners have been doing it for decades and there is not a single recorded case of anything going south. Why would I feel the need to tell you that? Because I have witnessed many examples of people whose emotions and feelings open up so freely and wildly that they get scared of their own energy!

That is common, and you are likely to go through a whole gamut of sensations during the breathwork. Make a choice to stay with them all and keep exchanging. I promise it will lead you to a profound spiritual experience.

I see the breathwork meditation as a condensed replica of our whole life. Yes, I mean that. Everything that we keep running into during our days, we'll experience during a single breathwork session. For example, if we are prone to disliking loud rock music, we're bound to be distracted by the music that accompanies the meditation. If we hate people imposing and disrupting our inner peace, there will be someone (even if only a memory) intruding on our meditation.

In short, there will be trouble. You'll get annoyed, doubtful, scared, angry, or sad. You'll resist the breath fiercely and may reach a point when everything in you will be demanding that you cease the practice immediately.

Now, the trick is not to.

As in your life, so in breathwork—and vice versa. As you learn to enhance your consciousness, you will awaken from the resistance when you see it for what it truly is: an attempt of the mind to control the experience.

There is no greater and more direct method to train your awakening or to enhance your consciousness than the breathwork meditation, in my humble opinion. During the active phase, which lasts roughly two thirds of the total meditation time, the above mentioned resistance will test you in every which way.

Awaken from the grip of resistance.

There is a simple common denominator to all those various kinds of resistance: the dimming of consciousness. Almost as if you were in a nightmare, you may fall prey to a single element of your own old story which will blind you to its real power—or lack thereof—and take over your whole experience.

You will fear that element, whatever it is. You may run away, fight, or resist it. And you know what they say: resistance is futile. In this case, resistance is not only futile, it is the very force that blocks your healing progress. The more you resist, the more stuck you get. As the saying goes, what you resist, persists.

Training of enlightenment

There's good news. Just as you can awaken from a nightmare and instantly free yourself from the perceived power it had over you, so too can you awaken from your resistance during breathwork. You can awaken from whatever belief you want or need to resist. This awakening is key.

It is an actual moment of enlightenment. No matter how tiny, such shards of awakened awareness work together in synergy and "their combined effect is greater than the sum of their individual effects," just as the dictionary says. Not only do we gradually gather and linearly collect all the times we awaken from our resistance, we also connect and string them together in a way that defines a brand new story, a new leaf we turn in the book of our lives.

As in breathwork, so in daily life.

So the more resistance we encounter during our breathwork, the better our chances to enhance our consciousness. When we start looking at it that way, we may become able to welcome not only the hard times during our meditation practice, but the hard times in our daily lives. We may learn to sincerely smile at them, knowing fully well they are harbingers of change for the better. And as you probably realize, that's a huge step on our path to healing.

During a recorded breathwork session, I will support and lead you as an intuitive voice, reminding you to keep relaxing and choosing to generate ever more trust and self-love in your heart. I will repeat that your one and only task is to stay with the two-stage breathing pattern and that alone will demand of you to remain entirely present, or conscious, at all times.

If you slip and return to a normal breathing pattern, that's okay. It happens to practically everybody almost every time. No matter what happens and no matter what you feel—and how you feel about it—simply resume your two-stage rhythm commitment. That's all there is to it. No need to stop and think about it. Keep focusing your attention to the breath and your feelings.

The loving power of the breath

The beauty and magic of breathwork lies in its utter and natural simplicity. All you really need to do is to breathe and stay conscious. True, sometimes that's easier said than done, but still. Like the elegance of chess with its plain rules and complex play combinations, breathwork works miracles without you having to understand its underlying principles.

I assure you: if you learn to stay present with the breath for the whole duration of the meditation, you will learn to stay present and at the place of self-love in your daily life amidst the emotional storms and rough patches that invariably happen.

Self-love is key to healing.

The breathwork will test you and train you. It will bring up all that's been buried within you, lying dormant, blocked, forgotten yet not forgiven. The breath will open your heart and create space to generate self-love. It will invigorate and motivate you to release the flow once again. Its built-in intent will guide you internally to open up to Spirit—and when your soul and Spirit meld and work together, no other control is needed, or wanted.

The free-will choice

Only about 7 minutes of conscious breathing is needed for the mind to either relax or revolt. Which of the two happens is—in my opinion—decided by Spirit, or your soul. It is beyond anyone's control. I would support you at this point and avoid any attempts to direct the healing. We will exercise free will in its clearest form, and choose to trust the healing process unconditionally.

If the mind resists, it may be time for release. Let's follow that lead. Instead of succumbing to the resistance and fighting the triggers and effectively ourselves, let's open and warm up to the possibility of something unknown and new.

Follow Spirit's lead.

When your consciousness is ready, you'll awaken from your ordinary, nightmarish reactions caused by the resistance. You will instantly realize, on the level of feelings and awareness, that something fresh and interesting is underway. You will see your chance and choose to seize it. You will choose your healing.

Your resistance can be anything that you will deal with at that moment: from simply having to sneeze or scratch your nose, to having a hard time swallowing or taking in breaths, to wondering whether your breathing pattern and rhythm are correct, to feeling there is something bad going on and that everything in your life is falling apart, and it's your fault, and you're powerless to prevent it. The scenery of the illusion can be anything at all—but the point is simple and singular: it's just an illusion!

You are powerful beyond words, numbers, comparison, or measure. Your power is the power of love. The power of trust. The power to create anything you want to focus your attention on. The power of Spirit working through you as your soul enters your body.

The vibration of the soul

There will come a time when all of your blocks will be melted away, all of your trapped emotions released, all of your resistance used up as fuel for self-love—and all that's left will be your soul singing and dancing in your heart, body, and energy field.

This is not a black & white event, but an ongoing process. There is always something more to everything, or else life would be boring. But as soon as your mind learns to relax enough to let go of some control—and that can surely happen during your first try!— you will experience something novel in your life: a gentle tingling sensation in your hands and arms, or a soft quivering in your heart, or a pleasant electrical charge in your feet and legs. You will feel shivers running up and down your spine—and then some. Your whole body might feel as if on fire or electrified!

Witness your soul flowing into your body.

I call that the vibration of the soul. It is the interpretation we feel on the physical level when the soul enters, or starts to enter, our body. The truth is that this vibration is always there, but we can't perceive it in our ordinary mode of cognition, because the mind is too loud and grabs and completely occupies all of our finest attention. But as long as we live, and breathe, the vibration is there, within: a divine spark to animate otherwise dead matter.

It is this spark of Spirit consciousness that does the healing in our lives, if we only let it, and get out of its way. Since the vibration is ever present, our body and our whole being has the capacity of self-healing. And when we are conscious of it, it works even better—because where attention goes, energy flows. Hence the acceleration of healing that breathwork brings about as we practice it consistently.

The healing phase

The last third of the meditation is done passively, breathing naturally, through the nose or through the mouth, one breath in, one breath out. The recording will lead you to shift from the active to the passive, resting, or healing phase.

> Revert to natural breathing and recharge.

Just rest and recharge your batteries.

Your mind goes to nothing and yet you remain completely present with all of your feelings, emotions, and even thoughts that are floating around without disturbing you in the slightest. That's unconditional acceptance par excellence.

You are…

Nothing more.

Not controlling anything.

Simply observing everything.

Letting your soul—or your higher self—do the work in collaboration with Spirit.

All the generated self-love, joy, and peace—in the form of vibration—permeates your energy field and unravels the mystery of your experience, outside the limitations of space and time. Past traumas are addressed and released, even the old ones belonging to your family lineage. Future worries and fears are softened and let go from your focus, forgotten to the point of pure disinterest.

Your complete whole is concentrated in the here and now, where the power of love is.

Spontaneous emotional releases may still occur in this phase and they are always powerful. You are remaining neutral, seemingly unaffected. A spiritual momentum is building.

Here is where the long-term, lasting, sustainable healing happens.

The manifestation

At this stage, the intent you set up at the beginning of your session or extended practice will take hold, grow roots, and blossom. Bring your pure awareness to it now. Fuel it with all that you are. As soon as you sense the realness of it, it will manifest. Time-travel to that moment from your vision in the future when it has already manifested.

> Feel your intent has already manifested.

You may get visions of specific steps to take in your life. Note them. You will have a chance to jot them down after the meditation—but if you urgently feel you have to write them down right now lest you forget, do it immediately. Be clear and sober enough to know whether it's just your mind trying to control you by misleading you, or whether it's the heat of your true intent spurring you into direct, creative action.

Conversely, if your visions and ideas of new steps on your path to healing frighten you or make you feel despondent and unable to

fulfil your own expectations or to realize your innermost dreams—
be aware that this is the mind's resistance speaking up again, trying
hard to retain a foothold in a foundation you're building from
scratch.

To the mind, your immense adventure of following the flow of
Spirit seems absurd and downright scary. It will do its best, or
worst, to keep protecting you, even from yourself. Right at this
point, you will see with clarity the many deceptions and delusions
of the mind. Any feelings and emotions that arise during this stage
are where your next cycle of healing lies. Welcome them and don't
deny them—their presence is invaluable if your desire to heal
yourself is sincere.

Even through the fog of resistance, you can hope for a glance of
how your visions and dreams will still come true and manifest in
your life!

Return to your body

At the very end of the meditation, you'll be guided to ground
and return to your body fully. You'll start doing that at your feet, by
wiggling your toes. Then you'll proceed upwards over your lower
legs and knees all the way to the hips. You can gently sway left-to-
right here and continue upwards. Sense the internal organs and
just notice how you feel in general.

Realize where you are—in your body and in your room—as you
progress upwards and reach your neck and perhaps turn your head
a bit. Feel into your arms and hands and now wiggle the fingers too.
At last, feel your face, smile, and gently open your eyes.

And you're back. Welcome.

Ground.

Before you get up and resume your daily routine, make sure you're up for it. If the breath took you deeply into Spirit, you might feel groggy or unstable. Be careful and patient. That's also an aspect of your self-love.

If you want you can apply the grounding practice here to return to your normal self and life.

Notes of your sacred visions

Anything that may have come to you during the breathwork, write it down. Look at it as an exercise in creativity. You don't have to understand it or control it in any way. Flow with it. Later on we'll connect this to the element of *creative writing*.

Onwards ho!

After you've been exchanging with breathwork for some time in your life, your consciousness will emerge and rise in ways nobody could imagine—using the mind alone. Spirit will routinely accompany you at your daily tasks, and desirable synchronicities will follow you around. Your intuition will be powerful and trusting it will be a cinch. You will realize how natural it has become for you to base your choices—even the most crucial ones—on what your inner compass of the soul is telling you in the heart, through the language of the vibration. Yes, you will start to feel the vibration more and more often even outside of your breathing practice.

Before long, your life will be changed. A new kind of hope will well up from your soul, one that will never leave you again.

Your life starts now.

Enjoy!

Cheat Sheet: Breathwork Meditation

START

#1 — Make sure nobody will disturb you

#2 — Lie down on your back and relax

#3 — Put on the meditation recording

#4 — Set the intent for the session

#5 — Do the active phase of the breathwork:

- focus on your body and feelings

- breathe through the mouth only

- two breaths in and one breath out

- breath 1 in the lower abdomen

- breath 2 in the upper chest

- exhale, and repeat

#6 — Switch to the passive, or healing, or resting phase:

- breathe naturally through the nose or the mouth

- one breath in and one breath out

- keep resting and recharging

- feel your desired intent being manifested

#7 — Return to your body and ground

#8 — Write down any insights or visions you had

↓

BREATHWORK MEDITATION

Creative writing

Ah, creative writing!

Not something everyone likes, I'm sure. But why? Any kind of creativity could be the ultimate expression of our originality and freedom as human beings. Being creative is the closest to becoming a god, a creator.

> Creativity is Spirit acting through you.

If you are an artist or creative in your own right, connect that to your healing process and bring it in. As a writer, I composed the ONE MOON PRESENT formula to work with creative writing specifically. Even if you're not a writer, I promise you that using this tool will open up the doorway to joy and peace in your life.

We will use any resistance to creative writing, should it appear, as fuel for more self-love. Remember that we're doing this because we want to—it is our choice.

It is amazing to me that many cringe at the mention of creative writing and fear overwhelms them. But you can look at creative writing as an invitation to do as you please, no expectations, no limitations, no rules—just make something up and write it down. By definition, you can't go wrong with it no matter what you do. But we are scared of that. Scared of total freedom. Seems strange, but considering how our subconscious programming works, it actually makes perfect sense that we are afraid of our own power and success.

As with the other tools of the healing formula, I kindly invite you to suspend your judgment and perform the delineated tasks in your own manner. It will be easy and fun!

Just briefly, to placate the mind minimally: why creative writing? How can that assist you to deal with hard emotions and hard times in the real world?

Well, you wouldn't be reading these lines if you didn't believe in Spirit in one way or another. You are aware, on some levels at least, that the universe is not linear and purely logical. You may very well intuit your true nature as a creator.

What you focus on, you create and sustain.

A caveat here. Most of what we focus on is determined by our subconscious programming. That's where our *chi*—our life force—flows daily. What is left of it at the end of the day is often barely enough to keep us alive.

Creative writing is more than just scribbling down words and sentences. It all starts with profound clarity and conscious observing. Doing that—together with practicing the other components of the ONE MOON PRESENT formula—will help us see through the fog of our denial and resistance. It will undo the knots that hold in place the veil of our old programmed story.

Our tasks of creative writing will be two-fold: to track our current or pre-existing condition, and to navigate ahead. With the former we embrace our past and with the latter, our future. As we heal to our completeness, they meet in the present.

Captain's Log

First, I invite you to meticulously log, record, and transcribe all of your present states of mind, emotions, and feelings. By that I simply mean you will jot down in plain terms *where you are at*, every day at a certain time of your choice. Let's call that record *a captain's log*.

I suggest you pay close attention to your body position and feelings, as that is the basis of our worldly existence. Write down in your captain's log if you notice anything out of the ordinary, or anything ordinary to the point of uncanny repetition.

For example, if you wake up with a terrible headache, log that. If you feel a pang of pain behind your left shoulder blade when you put on your t-shirt, log it. If you develop a nasty itch on your right ankle one fine afternoon, jot it down. Also notice your constant slouching which accompanies the feeling of unrest in your shoulders. And write down how often you don't feel your feet are touching the ground. Maybe you can feel a certain disconnection in your knees as well, or even in your stomach. Ultimately, you'll be able to connect all the separate dots.

Next, follow up with any emotional patterns you perceive and can track through time. Either log in every fluctuation of your emotions as they arise or record a series of them as a whole. Or both. Anything goes. Be inspired. Get creative.

Write honestly about who you are and were.

When it gets really tough and you don't feel like showing up—make a small effort and mark that down at least symbolically: just write a tiny minus sign in the log if you're absolutely reluctant to translate into words. That's alright too. It still counts. It has tremendous value, believe me.

You can also write about your thought processes, but keep it short. Don't let it possess you and take control of your intuitive, creative side. Perhaps it's best to designate a time-frame such as five minutes, and write down whatever comes to your mind during that period, your *stream of consciousness*, as it's called in writer's circles—not to be confused with our definition of consciousness.

You can also write down anything you observe emerging as a pattern, such as a repeating thought-form or belief that you entertain often—whether you like it or not, agree with it or not. For example: life is hard; nobody loves me; something is wrong with me and the whole world. That's from my own captain's log.

Whenever you go deep during the breathwork meditation and old memories of past traumas surface, write that experience down as a full and proper captain's log entry. That's golden! The more detail you recall, the better for your healing. These pearls from your past are the missing dots, and are vital for connecting the complete mesh of your destiny. I include some of my own in the next chapter for your inspiration.

This aspect of your creative writing will assist you in grounding your feelings about yourself. It will show you the places where you still don't know how to love yourself. In conjunction with the breathwork practice, it will be a powerful tool of introspection. And the final tool in the toolbox, *learning self-love*, can help you address those points in your life.

Captain's Log Sample Entry

I feel confused. I'm afraid I can't finish all my tasks scheduled for today. I feel overwhelmed. Lost. Helpless. Frustrated. What should I do?

My vision is limited—I don't notice anything around me. I focus within and on my problems. My heart is beating only faintly. I'm slouching. I feel under pressure.

Where are my feet? I'm disconnected down there, empty.

My expression is serious. My lips are curled downwards. The jaw is clenched.

I feel trapped or stuck in my life. What can I do?

This has been repeating itself for months now. I constantly feel that I am not enough. I can't change my life…

Vision Chart

As you work with the One Moon Present formula and learn new aspects of self-love, creative writing will also serve to consolidate your new story. That is the other side of this potent tool of manifestation. Your creative juices can first soften and dismantle your old habits. Then, they can fertilize the grounds and nurture the fresh roots your visions and dreams need to grow strong and blossom.

You may keep notes that are separate from your captain's log. You may call them *a vision chart*. Again, exchange with it—even with the paper you write on or the computer document you use. Treat the whole process with utmost respect and feel it is your sacred ritual. The more you can sense that, the more spiritual magic you will create with it.

Jot down all your visions, dreams, revelations, and insights you get during meditations or at any other time. Don't be alarmed if Spirit wakes you up at 3am only to reveal yet another beautiful piece of the mosaic you're weaving. Make a conscious, joyful effort to write it down in your vision chart. Then again, if you're exhausted from your busy day and would like to appreciate a good night's sleep—that choice is also valid. Remember, you call the shots of self-love.

Every day, preferably at the same time, perhaps right after your daily breathwork practice, rally all the clarity and heart you can and write down your intent: where you want to go next. Envision and manifest the next step on your path. Leap into your full power. Grab the wheel of your destiny. You're the captain.

Make sure you get honest about everything that may prevent you from actualizing your full potential and realizing your innermost dream. These may appear as past traumas and trapped emotions, old family patterns of inadequacy and powerlessness, and fear of change and the unknown. Remember, nothing has to be difficult. Things get hard only when we overthink and resist, and it's always our own power that backfires and hurts us.

Take your time to imagine all the fresh ways you could love and support yourself unconditionally in your daily endeavors. Apply the *learning self-love* tool, which I describe in the following section. Write down the specifics—the more detailed, the better.

> Dare to dream your wildest dream.

In your heart—like during the breathwork practice—create space and trust so you can take a risk and believe that you *will* manifest all that you want! You are already manifesting it. The Universe listens to you and if you exchange with Spirit you can co-create everything.

Before you put down your vision chart, close your eyes and deeply feel how the wheels of fortune are spinning and your new reality is being created for you.

And that's the second aspect of creative writing: inventing the *after* story, or your new story. Together, both elements take care of changing your reality, in whatever way you see and understand that erase & rewrite process.

Instead of starting from scratch, you can take a story from your captain's log and rewrite it for your vision chart. That's not cheating. In fact, it's a powerful way of out-creating your old story by intending a new one. You can set your new stories as far into the future as you wish or as close to today as you dare—while staying present and grounded.

And you might be surprised how certain old stories are rewritten "by themselves", on the pages of your everyday life, when you are committed to your healing path. Such stories are neither *before* nor *after*, but *now* stories, and equally belong to the captain's log and the vision chart.

I'll share some more examples of my own in the following chapter and two short samples, original and raw, here.

Vision Chart Sample Entry #1: Out-creating the old story of the Captain's Log sample entry

I look around and remember: I have a choice. I smile. I embrace my feelings of helplessness, confusion, and not belonging here.

I'm aware of my wounded inner child, hurting because of past traumas. He is me. I love him and hold him tight and ask him for forgiveness for anything that I might have done wrong in this life. He feels loved, warm, and supported. I feel forgiven.

I feel my feet again, connected to Mother Earth through the floor of my room. There is a flow of energy. It rises up to my stomach and heart. I keep smiling. I feel great. Alive. Free.

I trust myself and Spirit. All will be accomplished in its time. There is no hurry, no pressure. I feel a flutter in my heart. That's the only thing that matters right now, at this moment.

I'm powerful and at peace. Life is good.

Vision Chart Sample Entry #2: A fresh vision as received during my breathwork meditation

I have a dream.

A man walks down a street. His heart is shining so bright that his whole body is illuminated. I can see a halo around him. His posture and movements are calm and humble. His eyes are focused on Life, Nature, and Mother Earth, even though he is in the midst of a big city. His posture is relaxed and expression serene as if he didn't have a problem under the sun. Yet a spark in his profound look speaks of compassion. He exudes a vibe of love. He is magnetically beautiful in a gentle and powerful way.

I realize: I am that man!

You'll see. Creative writing is pure magic! It will change your life and the way you look at yourself. Who knows, maybe you'll start to realize that you've always been a healer and a writer.

And finally, do you dare to talk with others about yourself being a creative writer or perhaps a healer? If you give it a try something monumental may shift in your perception of who you are and who you want to be.

That's not part of the practice—it's more like a cherry on top of the cake!

Cheat Sheet: Creative Writing – Captain's Log

START

#1 — Prepare sacred space and time

#2 — Invoke conscious clarity about your life

#3 — Create a new entry in your captain's log:

- write down *where you are at* generally

- describe your *body position* in some detail

- *track* your feelings, emotions, and thoughts

- transcribe your *stream of consciousness*

- detect and report any *repeating patterns*

#4 — Ground your feelings about yourself

THE BEFORE STORY

Cheat Sheet: Creative Writing – Vision Chart

START

#**1** — Prepare sacred space and time

#**2** — Sense the sparks of your creative magic

#**3** — Write down your new insights and visions

#**4** — Establish and inscribe your future intent:

- where do you want to go next?

- what is stopping you?

- how can you love yourself through the block?

- make up your new story, with specific details!

#**5** — Feel the manifestation already taking place

THE AFTER STORY

Learning self-love

What is self-love?

I believe there is no universal answer and the real question is "what is self-love *to you*?" Not only that—it's also vital that you *feel* the answer. *Your* answer.

Right now, I want you to pause and create three minutes of free time, and ponder about your particular kind of self-love and some aspects of it. Can you do that? Do you feel worthy and powerful enough to afford doing it? And most importantly, do you *want* to?

> You can generate self-love in your heart.

You see, even your choice right now to shift your priorities and unconditionally pause to feel your self-love—perhaps without a clear understanding how and why—can be an act of self-love. It may generate self-love.

My friend David likes to remind me, "The way we do anything is the way we do everything." We can encounter self-love in every single act, feeling, emotion, or thought. And in our every response to life.

If I had to use one general definition of self-love I'd say it is an unconditional embrace of your *wounded inner child.*

The wounded inner child

The wounded inner child is a part of us that is disconnected from our whole being. A past trauma or a rough experience we couldn't cope with caused our awareness to split. Healing is the process of reuniting our pieces and self-love is the super-glue.

Whenever we encounter a situation in life that resembles our original trauma, the wounded inner child gets triggered. We get lost in the diminished awareness of the wounded inner child, which is like a snapshot of our past consciousness. The mystery and nature of awareness is such that as we focus on the old memory, we become someone else in the present. We project the trapped emotions and negative expectations onto our reality in the now. The wounded inner child may be emotional in any way: belligerent, withdrawn, angry, sad, overwhelmed, resentful, or scared, and in a sense, we become the wounded inner child in that moment.

That's why a seemingly innocent event, like spilling a cup of tea, may cause profound disturbance and an unproportionally severe response of guilt, for example. Others can't understand your overreaction, for who else can know what happened to you after you spilled tea as a child and in the process broke valuable china or got seriously burned?

It is time your wounded inner child stops hurting.

Often, it is not about our own past traumas. Some rifts of awareness are inherited through a lineage and past lives. In any case, it is highly unlikely that we are fully aware of what is going on when we get triggered. We get dazed and confused. We are not ourselves.

In such instances, when we act as if we were someone else, our inner response to our outward reaction may be antagonistic, because we can't accept the negative of our inner polarity. We are not okay with who we are in that moment. We judge it. We don't love ourselves. We don't love our wounded inner child, who suddenly appears to us as a foreign entity within our being. We want to get rid of that strange, unwanted part, but it is still a part of ourselves. And that is the opposite of self-love.

Ironically, even our urge to become someone else, someone better, someone perfect or complete—even this appetite for healing—can be motivated by our lack of self-love. That's why I stress this here: there is no true healing without self-love.

Becoming complete

Self-love entails unconditional acceptance of who you are even when you feel negative in any way—and especially then. I feel this aspect of self-love as if embracing my wounded inner child when he is suffering because of spilled tea or when he is afraid of any situation, no matter how innocent it may seem.

The power of self-love lies in being in two places—or two states—at once. Simultaneously I feel I am a helpless, suffering child being consoled, supported, and loved, while at the same time I sense myself as a powerful, caring, competent adult who pours all his love onto a child, the love of his life. Being present in both sentiments and states of consciousness at once is the unifying super-glue of self-love.

> Self-love is a state of being when you love a troubling
> part of yourself and feel loved unconditionally.

Now, I kindly invite you to open up another list, or document, titled *My Self-love*. Write down whatever you found out and felt about your self-love in those three minutes you created for yourself. How *do* you embrace your wounded inner child in the face of adversity?

Learning self-love is a purely practical exercise. I find many people have trouble realizing the difference between thinking about self-love and actually experiencing it; they are not the same. If you're honest about wanting your healing, you can vault directly to the practice of self-love: do something right now as a way of embracing your wounded inner child.

A simple example

Let me give you an example. I adore my nineteen-month-old toddler with his dark, joyful, curious, vibrant, all-knowing eyes and the sound of his high-pitched voice pointing out the mysteries of his world to me in a baby-semi-verbal way. He opens my heart.

But when I'm busy working and late for a deadline and I can't be bothered, his demanding, energetic presence distracts me and triggers in me a great fear of not being enough. My heart closes and I want to be left alone. Furthermore, my own response abhors and depresses me.

It doesn't matter why my wounded inner child reacts that way. What matters is that I awaken from the state of diminished awareness where everything seems dark and hopeless, and enhance my consciousness enough to remember the *learning self-love* tool—and use it immediately!

Embrace your wounded inner child.

I embrace all my negative feelings of not being enough and of not being a good father, while visualizing or sensing my wounded inner child. I feel compassion for him and offer him my unyielding support. I'm deeply aware of the rift in my being, yet also that the healing is underway—not merely a temporary relief, but a long-term process of becoming complete once again.

For me, this episode is something to jot down in the *My Self-love* journal. By keeping a record, I am becoming aware of who I am and I'm learning new aspects of my self-love. In this example, I learned that I can immerse myself in work and still be a great father—and I love myself for it.

Keep exploring what self-love is and how it feels to you. In what ways is your wounded inner child hurting and how can you embrace them? You can trust yourself to discover something new daily and add it to your ever-growing *My Self-love* list. All it takes is your sincere willingness to dedicate your time to it, and do the work.

When your day goes by without any suffering and you are grateful for that, you can still apply yourself to find at least one new aspect of your self-love—your own fresh definition of self-love.

For example, "I'm a good father even though I'm sometimes busy." Or, "I know I'm doing the best I can as a partner." Or, "Even when I'm exhausted from a hard day, I can still be kind."

You can find a new gesture or a new way of expressing your self-love in practice. This can be anything at all. Perhaps you need two hours to yourself and a lavender bath with candles. Perhaps you need to not eat the chocolate cake, or you do need to eat it, or maybe you need to back out of an engagement you made, forgive a family member, or kiss your reflection in the mirror with a mischievous grin. Perhaps your wounded inner child needs to go outside and climb a tree. The choice is yours alone. Nobody else can know that for you.

Self-love is a way to make your life fulfilled again. It also becomes the reason for wanting to live—the purpose for choosing to walk the path of a human being. Any path. Your path.

Do the work

Knowing that you can do it—that you can heal yourself—commit to doing this work for at least 28 days. Do as much as you can. Feel that you support your own choice, whatever it is. You've got your back, and you know you can count on that!

Using the breathwork and other tools, track the negative, abusive energies in your life or your lineage. Expose all the negative thought-forms and pessimistic beliefs that do nothing but make you miserable. You don't have to hate them—they are part of your legacy. But you don't have to keep them. The power of choice is yours alone.

If there is a lack of love in our lives, let's keep digging and we may find that love in the most unlikely places, such as under the masks and shields we use to escape reality. In a way, suffering and resistance are signposts to healing. Use them like a compass.

Remember, it is your wounded inner child who is suffering and waiting for your embrace. You are both waiting to be reunited by self-love.

I'm not saying you have to walk through fires. But you can use the map of your discomforts, fears, and other negativity in order to forge the easiest way across. Get clear around what is what, that's all. The tools of One Moon Present formula will help you reach clarity and grounding automatically, when you use them and exchange with them.

Commit to being there for you.

Healing comes to us when we are patient and willing to be at our worst and our best simultaneously. Even as we feel down, exhausted, and without a hope in the world, we sense the awakening of something infinitely stronger from within. Something true. We choose to trust that infinity in our heart, which is our soul and Spirit combined. We allow ourselves to experience it all, the heaven and hell, the human and divine, at the same time, equally, in a balanced manner, without leaning in any direction.

Find—no, *create* a way to unconditionally love your day, your life, your self, and it will all come together! You will learn to appreciate the endless mystery of awareness in action.

Cheat Sheet: Learning Self-Love

START

#1 — Feel what self-love is to you

#2 — Write it down in your log

#3 — Each day find another new aspect of self-love:

    - in what way is your wounded inner child hurting

    - how can you embrace your wounded inner child

    - be in both states at once: loving and being loved

#4 — Commit to trusting love and doing the work

#5 — Appreciate the mystery of awareness

SELF-LOVE

An example of a day on my healing path

In the snapshot of my typical healing day below, I omitted my "real life" schedule. One reason for that is to keep it simple and readable, but more importantly, I want to stress that ONE MOON PRESENT formula applies to all walks of life and ways of living. I trust you to fit it into your own busy schedule.

From as far back as I can remember, I've been practicing the marvelous tools of healing that I learned from many masters along the way. I combined and further developed the original tools through experience, and according to my nature and vision as led by intuition. I invite you to be inspired by my example, yet I strongly suggest that you trust your own ability as a healer and start tweaking and adapting any of it to your own personal preferences and circumstances.

After all, how boring would the world be if we all followed the same formula? This ONE MOON PRESENT formula is meant merely as a starting point, a catalyst of sorts to get you going—but may you learn to fly on your own as soon as possible. Generate your own trust, love, and wisdom and you will never have to seek it elsewhere again.

Good luck!

7:21	wake up and remember that life is good and I'm walking the path of healing
	…
7:34	(do yoga, tai-chi, tensegrity or similar exercises)
7:47	step outside onto the dewy grass and *ground*
	…
8:14	remember to *stay present* when putting on shoes
	…
9:00	use alarm to remind me to do a *quantum breath*
	…
2:00	use alarm to remind me to do a *quantum breath*
	…
3:54	remember to *stay present* when putting on shoes
3:56	learn a new aspect of my *self-love*
	…
5:13	embrace my wounded inner child when I feel hurt or scared
	…
6:15	use alarm to remind me to do a *quantum breath*
	…
7:06	do the *breathwork meditation*
7:20	do *creative writing exercise*
	…
9:15	use alarm to remind me to do a *quantum breath*

IV.   ENGAGE:
Healing can be fun!

You are not alone

What will inspire you to trust love, trust yourself, and do the work?

At first I wasn't sure how to structure this last, inspirational part of the book. My intention was to offer you some real-life examples of dealing with hard emotions and hard times. I decided I'll simply use my own true stories.

Their basic intention is to demonstrate that we're not that different at all. If I can create a new life story, so can you. But I realized I can offer even more. Perhaps I can inspire you to continue writing your captain's log and vision chart entries even beyond the one moon cycle?

What if you could write a book and inspire many others?

Let me claim that doing the exercises and your own healing work will help shift something in your life and make all the difference, even if you don't understand how or why. I talked enough about the theory in the previous chapters—if you skipped that part you can safely return to it now, or whenever it calls you.

In this chapter, I include a short selection of stories from my life that might appear quite common, perhaps even dull: my fear of going to the dentist, my road-rage, and my sadness at witnessing childhood poverty. The stories are based on my own healing notes.

I rewrote them as an author and as a healer. They honestly and transparently reveal those hard emotions I should by some standards be ashamed of—and so I was until I learned how to love myself through it all, shame included.

No, we're not all that different, you and I, and that goes for everybody else on this planet. I claim that we are all able to develop our consciousness to the point of freedom, of liberating ourselves from our own beliefs. My plain stories are patterns that might help you help yourself. Yes, there are others going through the same process as you!

How can you work with these inspirational stories?

They can be used as a theme to focus on when applying the ONE MOON PRESENT formula. Each story is composed of sections based on multiple entries from my *Captain's Log*, *Vision Chart*, and *My Self-love Journal*, and show a progression towards healing. They may inspire your hope that the shift is possible and that healing is a choice.

The *Captain's Log* is about our current condition and *old* story. It's the type of material we journal for the purpose of bringing in more clarity and eventually unmasking any denial. These are the *before* stories.

The *Vision Chart* sections contain the dream visions we want to navigate to and manifest in life. They are the *after* stories. In my case, some of them are the *now* stories. They have already come true for me.

When you read a *before* story, notice if anything similar happened to you. Or something quite the opposite. Maybe you will identify not with me but with another character in the story, one with a contrasting role perhaps.

Observe with clarity and sobriety all that the *before* story stirs and brings up in you. Ask yourself: what does it trigger in you? Or, almost trigger—a sentiment you know is lurking just under the surface, being hushed up or denied and even demonized for years or generations. What are you avoiding?

Cast your stories like spells!

Now here is your chance to become a healer *and* a writer. If any of your old memories resurfaced, grab your pen and write them down. Do it as part of your creative writing exercise. Faithfully transcribe your own story in as much detail as you can. You'll see, if you do this every day you'll end up with a book of your own pretty soon! I do encourage you to entertain that idea as a valid possibility.

Yes, I want you to use my stories as an inspiration to write your own book. Why not? Know that by inspiring others you inspire yourself and by healing others you heal yourself.

At this point, it's a great time to use the *learning self-love* tool. Apply it to your story. Re-create yourself. Then write your *after* story—the dream vision. Your new story.

Write it down carefully and with as much attention to details as you only can, then do it even better, juicier. Don't judge your skill. The best writers doubt their writing, it's a general rule. This is not about perfectionism and it's not a competition: it's about your healing. So if you're sincere in wanting it in your life, don't let the little problems like a bit of shame or a perceived inadequacy squander your valiant efforts. You just write and write and write, whatever comes in and through you. Love yourself through writing, by writing! After all, you write about yourself, the one you (learn to) love the most.

> Just write.

While the creative writing exercise pertains to your daily observations and insights, your commitment to creating a new life can be a larger, timeless task. You can revisit your past and review, or *recapitulate*, all the significant and memorable events of it, which will in turn set you free emotionally and energetically. And you can dream yourself forward into your new life.

This is the magical, turning point, right here! This is where history is made, or the future, if you want to put it that way. I know you believe in healing because you're reading this—and know: *this* is it. There is nothing else, or more.

More than being about the destination—or the path—healing is about choice. The turning point happens when we make the conscious choice to bring about a change in our lives. Whatever has been stuck and blocked and whatever we denied and resisted, the knots will be undone when we focus on them with self-love and awareness.

The only element needed for us to shift from *before* to *after* story is a sincere and grounded choice to heal!

Healing does come when we create clarity and neutrality around our problems in life—after that, our focus naturally runs to what attracts our hearts: the beauty of life, peace, joy, and that is how we learn self-love and nurture it, day after day. The rest will follow. The mind will be relaxed, the emotions will flow freely, and the body will heal itself. That's all there is to it. Healing is our birthright when we step out of our own way.

<blockquote>You were born free.</blockquote>

If you do this step with abandon and trust, like you do your breathwork meditation, I promise you, you will sense some enchanted reality shift unfold in front of your very awareness! That's the kind of magic I believe in, and count on. Work with it. See what happens. Be a child again. Explore. Let it control you, take you by the hand and heart. Yell with it, sing along. Smile. Everything is possible!

You need no more instructions. Break free and take the wheel. You are a healer. Go!

Stories

Love Yourself Through Fear

A Child and the Dentist

The dental operating light blinded me as I reclined in the leather chair. I fumbled in search of a safe resting place for my damp hands. I practiced opening and closing my jaws. The dentist was preparing her gear outside of my scope of vision.

Her steps approached.

Knots in my guts tightened.

She greeted me as a ten year old boy that I was, and reached in to adapt the backrest to my body size. Her expression was stern and she smelled of disinfectant and something unique to dentists offices: tooth dust, as I learned decades later.

"Don't be so tense," she instructed upon observing my clenched fists—of which I wasn't even aware. "Relax and take steady breaths. You're gonna be alright."

I closed my eyes, doing my best to loosen up despite my mounting fear. My heart was racing. I could feel it in my throat as I opened my mouth.

I was exposed.

"No need to grip the armrests so fiercely," the dentist reprimanded me. My fingers had violently clawed at the chair without my volition. I drew a deliberate deep breath and let go.

"Let's see what we have here."

I froze. *What was the worst that could happen?*

With a little round metal mirror in one hand and that dreadful spike in another, she checked my teeth one by one, reciting something unintelligible to her assistant. It was coded. I couldn't decipher the meaning, but it didn't sound good. I braced myself.

She replaced the tools with a resounding clang.

"We'll fix one of the bad ones today and leave the rest for your other visits." She instructed her assistant on what to prepare. It implied cementing, which meant… drilling!

Oh, no. My whole body went rigid.

"Hey, hey, it's going to be over before you know it!" She was a terrible liar. She sounded indifferent.

Cotton rolls filled up my mouth, stretching my cheeks and lips to a huge discomfort. I anticipated the worst. *What if something went terribly wrong? What if she drills too deep and hits the bone? What if she drills into the wrong tooth?*

That chair was a cage. A trap. I felt powerless. I didn't know what else to do, so I gave up.

"Open up wider," she ordered too casually.

The room was hot. The drill startled me. I hid my panic, swallowing hard. The buzz grew closer, then entered my head. It assailed my tooth. I cringed, taut as a string.

"No!" came the angry words. "Don't move! Just relax."

She drilled hard. My skull vibrated. My jaw felt about to break off. Tears rolled down my cheeks. I couldn't swallow all the saliva. The assistant sucked it out with the ejector.

It was exhausting. It was agony. I lost all my energy and stopped caring. I lost track of time.

Drill-cooling water sprayed my tongue and palate. The stench of tooth dust was suffocating. I fiercely prayed for the ordeal to be over.

The pain, I could live with. But please. I didn't want damage. Damage that nobody could repair.

Toothache

Coming of age, I decided to stay away from dentists and doctors.

At twenty-five I travelled the world. I stayed in a remote, artistic town in Mexico for months, when a most intense toothache visited unannounced.

Three days. My teeth, jaws, and head pulsated in pure pain. No room for sane thoughts. The only thing certain was that I'm not going to no dentist. *But what if I had to?*

Nothing helped. I tried ice packs. I gurgled hot tea. I chewed mint leaves. I meditated—but not really. I did my best not to think about the possible consequences. *Was the tooth rotting alive?*

Hours upon hours, I stared at the white-washed ceiling, or green-tiled floors, fighting tears, moaning and begging for somebody to help me. Yet I didn't want help. The indecision was driving me mad.

I burrowed my head in the soft, silk pillow. Such pain, but I kept suffering, because I was controlled by fear. *I was never going to the dentist again.*

Only one problem: I was afraid of *not* going almost as much.

The ache went away as suddenly as it arrived.

A Real Nightmare

My recurring nightmare was of a tooth falling out. The sense of an irreversible damage still scared me to death.

One day, I had lunch at the office with my friend Marko. We chatted away. The food was bland.

I took a bite and felt one of my teeth was loose! Cold sweat ran down my spine. *Maybe it was a false alarm?*

Cloaking my fear from Marko, I kept re-checking my tooth while pretending to eat and listen. My guts trembled. *Nah, it was okay.*

Another chunk of old chicken and a tragedy occurred. My tooth fell out with a sinking feeling in the pit of my stomach! *Was this another nightmare?*

I had tunnel vision. I struggled to wake up, like so many times before. Not this time. *It wasn't a dream. It was real!*

My friend still suspected nothing. With stealth, I located the tooth within the mouthful of food and wrapped it in the paper napkin. *I'd inspect it later, alone.*

With the tip of my tongue, I felt a huge, gaping hole in my gums. A weakness came over me. I had to struggle to keep it together. Perspiration formed on my brow.

Unease messed with my intestines. *Would I be able to avoid seeing the dentist? What was the damage?*

It dawned on me that I'd just lost the tooth which gave me hell in Mexico some years before. It did rot in my mouth to the point of falling out. *What did I do?*

The denial was great. Fear soon subsided and I learned to live with a gap in myself.

The Healing

My friend Dunja praised her dentist to the skies. "He knows what he's doing. He's new school. And he's super patient and caring with his clients. I never feel any pain."

Why would you even go to a dentist? I changed the subject. But later that night, I considered her words. It was as if two distinct voices carried an argument within me.

— *Maybe it's time?*

— *Forget it! Too dangerous!*

— *But what if I did this? What's the worst that can happen? Well, I may suffer a little…*

— *Stop. The real problem is: what if they make it worse than it is, irreversibly so?*

— They know what they're doing. The guy's a pro.

— I will be at their mercy!

— But…

— No. I can't go there. There's no way for me to visit that dentist and have him tinker with my teeth!

— But, wait. What is it I really want? I mean, am I being absolutely honest with myself here?

— ???

— Come on. This is important. I know it is.

— OK, what? I'm listening, I am.

— Well, don't I want to be healthy? Will I let my old, childhood fears keep me stuck at a place where I don't want to be anymore?

— …

— Stop denying it: I'm just scared!

— It's true. But… It's not only fear, I explained that already: I don't trust them to do a proper job!

— Exactly, and that's where I'm stuck! It's not about the fear, or the pain, or the irreversible damage, is it? It's about trust. That's my issue right here. I don't trust anyone…

As soon as the two voices of my internal dialog merged into one single stream of consciousness, I relaxed and yielded. Something larger than myself seemed to take over. Crystal clarity enveloped me. I knew, without a doubt. I'd go to the dentist.

Free at Last

Waiting room. The smell coming from the dentist's office was still the same. So specific—no other place smells like tooth dust.

Last minute panic hit. Ants crawling in my belly, palms sweating, vision narrowed to posters with dental hygiene information for children. But I stayed present. It was my choice.

I took a deep breath to settle my restless legs and sat down on the wooden chair.

A guy in his thirties and an elderly woman seemed so comfortable, as if waiting for take-out. I didn't know where to rest my damp hands. I started to read David Elliott's book, *Healing*, to distract, or support myself. It didn't work.

I thought of leaving. I was free to change my mind.

Was I?

No. I was committed to my healing. I honestly wanted to fix my teeth and to address my resistance and trust issues.

I remembered: I now have the capacity to give myself all the support I need. I was learning self-love. I could feel my wounded inner child was scared and hurting. So I did it: I embraced him. I felt a flutter in my chest. Healing was underway.

Fear, distrust, negativity—none of that was my enemy, nor was it the battlefield. It was part of my experience and part of me.

The door to the dentist's office opened. I flinched. Other patients looked over as I rattled my chair.

The nurse called my name in a clear, strong voice. "Lesjak?"

Swallowing hard, I grabbed my book and followed her in.

The dentist had intelligent-looking brown eyes. He smiled knowingly, which helped me relax—to a degree. Yet I could still feel the large part of the iceberg of fear underneath the surface. It didn't matter. I trusted the process. I was doing it. I sat down in the chair.

He told me to open my mouth up wider. My fingernails dug into the leather arm holders.

"It's okay. Just relax."

His voice was almost indifferent, and history repeated itself: nobody seemed to genuinely care about me. I felt vulnerable, exposed, at the mercy of somebody else. I did not belong. This world was not safe.

However, this time, I refused to believe that. I was choosing to create a completely different story. My *new* story.

I opened wide.

I hugged my wounded inner child.

I relaxed and kept relaxing—and tensing again, like a yo-yo—for the duration of my visit.

It was hard, but it was my choice. I was no helpless victim. I knew what I was doing. There are no shortcuts, but I was taking the most direct route: the path of healing.

I trusted love. The world was safe.

Love Yourself Through Anger

One-way Street

The street narrowed from two-way to one-way. A blue-colored traffic sign with a white arrow signaled my right-of-way. Nevertheless, I realized some cars coming from the opposite direction had arrived before me and I had no problem letting them by. I was in no particular hurry.

As the last of the queue passed me, I started to drive, but I noticed yet another car incoming which apparently wanted to seize the chance and force its way. I continued on with confidence. I was doing the right thing. I was expecting the other driver to realize that and stop to give way. He didn't.

I gripped the steering wheel.

He drove as far as he could, then stared at me as if *he* couldn't believe *my* stubbornness: why wouldn't I allow him to pass? I allowed the others before him.

I ground my teeth.

The difference, pal, was that you came much later and should have waited at your red traffic sign fairly and squarely. I could never stomach people who deemed themselves something more and above the rules.

My heart raced and my palms grew sweaty.

I was standing for myself and for the little man against the exploiting elite—as I saw it. My rigid resolve was a sheer force twisting through my belly and guts. Nothing could move me, there was no turning back. I WAS RIGHT. I turned into an angry ox, a mulish, stubborn donkey. I glared at the driver, my rage burning in my eyes, meeting his gaze.

With a smile that was more like a grimace, I tried to mask my terror.

For yes, I was afraid—I had no idea who I was dealing with. For all I knew, he could be violent, aggressive, armed—or connected to high places. But I had decided: I was not backing off. No way.

He stepped out of his car all red in the face like a huge lobster. Coming closer, he waved to me frantically to move away as if shooing a mosquito.

Excusez moi!

My blood boiled over. Vision blurred, I forgot to breathe.

What frigging arrogance! Did he own the world or what?

I didn't care. A line was drawn in stone. Just wait and you'll see. Try me. I dare you. See how crazy I can get.

I could have been cool about it. If he calmly told me he was in a hurry and had a hard-time driving in reverse, and kindly asked me to move, I'd be glad to do it.

But not this way, oh no. You crossed the boundary of "no more mister nice guy".

He reached to open my car door.

I got scared.

No, not scared of him. Scared of myself and of what I could have done to him if I reacted the way I felt pushed to.

Garnering my self-control, I opted for a passive aggressive approach. I locked my door and switched off the engine. I took my phone and showed it to him.

No, we weren't going anywhere until you moved. And we could always call the police. I communicated all that without a word.

I observed myself getting into something quite unlike me. That was not who I was. Why was I doing that? I had to! It was my duty: a fight for justice, for the cause, for all the oppressed who didn't dare to face the insensitive bullies.

But I didn't feel right. I was all in my head, in my ideas, in my being right. I couldn't feel my body, except my pain and my bile, and my accelerated heartbeat.

I resented my own anger.

To aggravate the matter, quite a number of vehicles had gathered behind our cars in both directions. I thought of the saying "the clever one gives in," but I chose to be the stupid one in this case. This was it. The moment of truth. Good versus evil, and I was the good. I stood my ground. I was not budging.

The man seemed on the verge of exploding with rage. He spent a few minutes fuming and cursing at me and he kicked my car several times. Then he produced his own phone from his pocket, but upon realizing I wasn't even paying attention to him, he gave up.

Just like that, he was all done, as if his batteries ran out of juice.

I watched him closely. My rage was spent too.

Without a second glance, he turned on his heels and went back to his car. Of course, now he had to wait for all the other cars behind him to back up. But within seconds, the road was clear. I started my car and drove forward nonchalantly. No one wagged a finger at me. I felt like a victor.

But was I? Was I really standing up for myself and setting healthy boundaries? Or was I merely reacting to the programming of my old story?

Two-lane Freeway

A two-lane freeway. Not much traffic. As I was passing a line that had formed behind a truck, an expensive-looking car appeared in my rearview mirror and tailgated me. Ugh.

I saw two options. I could slow down and move over to the right lane or I could accelerate and stay in my lane. My foot hovered. It was nervous to take action.

On the one hand, braking and yielding humbly was not my cup of tea. I was not like that. Velocity was in my veins and I got itchy driving below the speed limit. But I was also not going to race and risk a ticket or worse, just because someone seemed to be in a hurry.

Pressure pounded at me. Annoyance elevated it. Then anger poured through my body in seconds. I didn't want to choose between a rock and a hard place. I swallowed hard.

I drove on. I sensed the driver's anger at me, and my own was simmering. I hated being in someone's way. They resented me for it. I knew it. I resented them, and I resented myself for allowing anger to get the better of me. My stomach cramped.

The red car advanced closer as if wanting to push me off the road. My tension mounted by the second and I realized I was clenching my teeth. I couldn't take this for much longer. I gripped the steering wheel, no—my *rage* gripped the steering wheel.

I had no choice: I had to make a choice. The confusion befogged my judgment. I was angry but I didn't want to be. I felt powerless. This was a no-win, no-win situation.

I struggled to resume control.

But I couldn't.

I felt threatened, overwhelmed, as if I had entered a surreal nightmare. Why was this happening to me?

Defiant, my eyes glazed over. I gaped at the other driver in the rearview mirror. He seemed oblivious and impatient.

No: I was not backing off. I'd done that my whole life. No more. Why should I always give in to the expectations of others? My jaw was tense. Behind me, the red car bobbed up and down on the uneven road.

Stubbornly, I kept driving with unchanged speed, but my indecision grew as my breath constricted. I felt worse and worse, as if I was committing the most heinous, criminal act. I slouched and stared at the road with tunnel vision.

I was mad at the driver—as if *I* was driving behind him and *he* didn't want to move over. I realized how upside down that was. Did I feel the need to prove to somebody I was in the right—and why? I glared at the rear mirror. Who did he think he was?

My heart raced. I pressed my lips together. Where was all this anger coming from? I didn't want to be this way!

I was burning with frustration, feeling incapable of taking action, frozen like a rabbit in headlights—even though I was the one who had a choice. *Two* choices. So where was the real problem? What was wrong with me and the whole situation? I didn't know. My left foot was pressing against the floor with mad force.

I couldn't take it. I jumped on the gas pedal and overtook the few remaining vehicles on the right lane, then slowed down and removed myself from the equation. I exhaled rage. I sacrificed myself. Again. Like always.

I hated myself. I lost: I lost control.

Love Yourself Through Sadness

Broken Glasses

The grey sky was dense. Monumental clouds pressed down and rendered the world a darker and colder place. The red diesel bus negotiated a turn, coughing and wheezing. The passengers leaned to find balance. With reluctance, I placed my hand on the worn green seat upholstery. I didn't feel safe touching anything in an unclean place.

The road was bumpy. A few raindrops left from this morning's shower swirled around on the window. They trickled down and out of sight. A row of beech trees brought life to bleak buildings clustered around a concrete desert. I imagined the people living there and some of their personal drama. Coming from a hamlet on the outskirts of town, I almost felt sorry for city folk.

A tiny playground grabbed my attention. A couple of boys sat in a sandpit. We drove closer and I noticed they must be twins, three or four years old. They played with twigs and wood chunks. They looked pale. I found their expressions too distracted for their young age—almost sorrowful.

Their oversized shorts and t-shirts seemed like hand-me-downs from an older sibling or cousin. The boys had short hair and wore glasses with thick brown plastic frames. I would hate wearing glasses.

The bus driver shifted to a lower gear, getting ready to accelerate away. Just then, the boy with his back towards me turned around. I realized his glasses were broken. Somebody had fixed them with a piece of bandage strip. Sadness sank my heart like lead.

Something moved through my chest. With my sleeve I wiped away a tear. Another turn of the road, and the boys were a memory, etched in my heart.

I Have a Dream

Sadness loomed over me for the longest time.

But I had a dream.

A man walked down a street. The street was commonplace, with a grocery store at the corner of a residential block and a park on the opposite side. Few trees offered sought after shade at high noon.

The man's gait was casual, almost absent-minded. His body was lean and fit and he walked and rocked as if he had soft springs in his knees. He smiled to himself and to a flock of pigeons searching for bread crumbs outside the park gates.

There was a halo around him. I could see it. His whole body was illuminated by the bright shine of his heart. His eyes were two rotating, blue and green supernovas.

He moved nimbly in a calm and humble posture, focusing on Life and Mother Earth—even though in the midst of a metropolis. He communicated with Nature as he gazed up to the placid cerulean skies, and around at treetop canopies reaching down with luminous greenery.

His composure was relaxed and expression serene as if he didn't have a single problem under the great central sun or the whirling of planets and the birth of galaxies. Yet a spark in his profound look spoke of compassion unto the ages—all the ages and times and sufferings of planet earth and her dreaming children.

He exuded a vibe of love that was sent across time, across space, into the heart of hearts, to be reflected and redistributed to all without exception. He was magnetically attractive in a powerful yet gentle way.

He was otherworldly and still rooted firmly, grounded in the moment.

He smelled of cozy mystery. I loved that scent.

Then I realized: I was that man!

Curious to read more of my personal, real-life stories about fear and how I learned to love myself through it all following the *One Moon Present* formula? Order *Love Yourself Through Fear* now and use the momentum to dive deeper! (FREE 14-minute meditation included.)

lytf.studioblest.com

Glossary

These definitions are merely guidelines or inspiration to help you open up to a new-story point of view. Some are included to clarify the more obscure or less common terms (e.g. *wounded inner child*, *pranayama*, *claircognizance*) and some are listed to expand the standard definitions of well-known terms, which are used in the *One Moon Present* book and formula in a new or different way (e.g. *mind, awareness, mood*).

abuse — Any expression or experience stemming from diminished *consciousness* and lack of *self-love* resulting in unbalanced *exchange*.

awakening — A temporary expansion of your *awareness*. Exercising awakening by daily *meditation* will grow your potential for a heightened *consciousness*.

awareness — Your essence and the essence of all there is: the stuff your soul is made of. Also, your knowing of the world around you and your attention to it.

belief — A mind-based *thought* form that focuses your energy to uphold your *old story*.

block — An interruption of the flow of your life energy, usually a consequence of a past trauma or inherited pattern of behavior. *Consciousness* softens and releases blocks.

breathwork — A central tool of the ONE MOON PRESENT formula. Daily practice of breathwork will help you nurture your *awareness* and *self-love*. The breath, when you *exchange* with it, carries the gentle yet unstoppable power of softening your emotional *blocks* and restoring your energy *flow*.

chi (or life force) — The energy flowing through your being for as long as you're alive. It can get obstructed or blocked. *Healing* restores its flow.

clairaudience — Intuitive hearing and speaking, based in the throat chakra, connected to the thyroid gland.

claircognizance — Intuitive knowing, based in the crown chakra, connected to the pineal gland.

clairsentience — Intuitive feeling, based in the heart chakra, connected to the thymus gland.

clairvoyance — Intuitive seeing, based in the third-eye chakra, connected to the eyes and the pituitary gland.

clarity — The opposite of *confusion.*

confusion — A mind-based perceived lack of sense, direction, and capacity for free-will choice. *Consciousness* clears confusion.

consciousness — A sublime, divine awareness of being aware, a state of being *awakened* or *enlightened*, a non-linear *presence* with all there is, externally and internally.

control (or the mind's control) — A tendency of the *mind* to protect your being by trying to direct absolutely everything.

creativity — A direct route to *healing* by transcending your *beliefs* and using *intuition* as the compass of your *soul* to guide your *free-will* choices and create your *new-story reality.*

denial — A natural mechanism for coping with an unbearable experience. May impede the process of *healing* when exaggerated. *Consciousness* exposes denial.

ego — An identification with anything less than the whole of who you are. Tightly coupled with the *mind*, the ego personality works tirelessly to protect itself—and you—against countless potentially harmful *beliefs*. May convince you to obsessively focus on fear, anger, or sadness and thus expend most of your daily energy for upholding your *old story* instead of creating healing in your life.

emotion — A movement of energy in your nervous system and your field of energy. Emotions can get stuck and may *block* your *flow* of *chi*, resulting in chronic fatigue, stress, discomfort or illness.

energy — The underlying source of all material existence, as opposed to *awareness*, the underlying source of energy, but also of non-physical existence.

enlightenment — Clarity and *presence* of awakened *consciousness*. The practice of ONE MOON PRESENT tools gives rise to frequent, tiny, quantum enlightenments.

exchange — Your *awareness* of the interconnecting *flow* of all there is. A sacred willingness to expand and open up to life, even in the midst of *resistance*. Giving and receiving freely of the essence of yourself, others, and the Universe. An unbalanced exchange *blocks* the *flow*.

feeling — A physical, bodily sensation, as opposed to an *emotion* based in your energy field and the nervous system. Feelings, emotions, and also thoughts are tightly coupled.

flow (or energy flow) — A natural state of all existence. When your flow is obstructed or *blocked* by stuck *emotions*, past traumas, or inherited *programs*, you experience a rift in *consciousness* where your *wounded inner child* gets disconnected from the whole, and you may need *healing*.

free will — Your soul-based capacity for making *choices* and creating *reality*. Can be obscured and confused by programming, patterns of behavior, and denial. *Consciousness* reveals and illuminates free will.

God — A common name for an unknowable source of all there is. *Spirit, Universe*.

gratitude — A direct route to *healing* by opening your heart, learning *self-love*, and balancing your *exchange* through appreciation.

grounding — A sacred ritual of pausing and connecting to *Mother Earth* and soul-based *reality*.

healing — A process of improving the quality of your life by learning who you are and how to love yourself.

humor — A direct route to *healing* by opening up to the *flow* and letting go of *control*.

inspiration — An avenue of soul-based communication that can be freely used against all odds, even through your worst mind-based *confusion*, *denial*, and *resistance*. *Breathwork* is an avenue to inspiration.

intent — An unknowable force of manifesting reality which you can't control but you can still use it in a mysterious way, especially during meditation.

intuition — A soul-based language of conscious *creativity*, as opposed to mind-based *thoughts*. A limitless, irreducible, and infallible expression of your *free will*. Your *soul* may intuitively communicate to and through you in many ways; also see *clairaudience*, *clairvoyance*, *clairsentience*, *claircognizance*.

love — A *state of being*, neither a *feeling/emotion* in the belly nor a *thought* in the head. Can co-exist with any feelings, emotions, and thoughts at the same time.

manifesting — Creating your reality by focusing your energy. It can be a *free-will* choice of opening up to and bringing in more *healing*, *love*, and universal *exchange* of Oneness, or a mind-based choice, upholding the diminished reality of your *old story*.

meditation — Any consistent and dedicated practice of *grounding* and relaxing the mind, and opening up to faith and your *soul* entering your body.

mind — A complex energetic organ of perception with the capacity of creating a virtual, mind-based reality, as opposed to a true, soul-based one. Neither negative nor positive, it can and usually is usurped and programmed by the stuck energies of past traumas to keep creating a mind-based *old story* of *suffering*.

mood — A current, inner response to your *feelings, emotions, thoughts*, and *state of being*. Also, a response to other responses in a layered fashion.

Mother Earth — A matrix for Humanity. A living, sentient being, unconditionally loving and supporting all living on Her.

negative — Anything we define by resisting it, fighting it, or running away from it.

new story — A story you create by choice to bring about a change in life.

old story — A story you repeat to yourself and which may keep you stuck in life.

pranayama — An ancient, yogic *meditation* technique based on conscious breathing, with countless variants.

presence — A conscious *clarity* about what is what, on the level of *awareness*, not thoughts.

prevalent mood — An overall response to yourself and life in general. A core building block of your *old (or new) story*.

quantum breath — A simple breathing exercise to train your *presence*. See the section on *staying present*.

reality — A relative and subjective manifestation that you maintain by focusing your attention. An interpretation of your internal and external perception. Either a mind-based construct, upholding your old story, or a soul-based conscious exchange with Spirit, opening your life to your purpose and fulfilment of your mission. Or an interplay of the two.

resistance — Any *feeling, emotion, thought*, or *mood* of *negativity*—or *positivity*—that may attempt to disrupt your process of *healing* by convincing you otherwise. *Consciousness* dispels resistance.

self-love — An unconditional embrace of your *wounded inner child*. A *state of being* when you love a troubling part of yourself and feel loved unconditionally.

soul — An inextricable aspect of *Spirit* pertaining to an individual being or many (potentially simultaneous) incarnations of a Being.

Spirit — An all-encompassing, eternal *awareness* and *consciousness* of all there is. *God, Universe.*

spiritual — An aspect of absolutely everything in life that is touched by the *reality* of *consciousness*.

state of being — A consequence of *awareness* flowing through our being, e.g. love, joy, peace. Sometimes confused with *feelings, emotions,* or *thoughts.*

suffering — A mind-based choice to diminish your experience against the free will of your soul.

thought — A unit of mind-based *energy* which can be focused in tune with your *free-will* choices or against them, thus accelerating or impeding your *healing* process.

vibration — A physical and energetic sensation of your *soul* or *Spirit* moving through your body and your being.

vicious circle — See *vicious circle. Healing* transmutes a vicious circle into a virtuous spiral.

wounded inner child — A part of you that is disconnected from your whole being as a consequence of a past trauma or a rough experience you couldn't cope with. When your wounded inner child gets triggered, your *consciousness* will shrink and your choices will be limited by *confusion, resistance,* and *denial.*

ONE
MOON
PRESENT

FREE Borut Lesjak starter healing kit

Subscribe to our newsletter at **onemoonpresent.com** to keep in touch and be advised of the forthcoming sequels and other goodies—get your **FREE Borut Lesjak starter healing kit**, including ONE MOON PRESENT **Quick Start Guide e-booklet & audiobook**, a **7-minute** ONE MOON PRESENT **breathwork meditation**, and the ONE MOON PRESENT **formula's beautifully designed set of cheat sheets**, as well as the first three books in the *Ink by Star* series of koans to awaken self-love. You will also receive an occasional, never-before published chapter from both behind the scenes, and from the great beyond.

If *One Moon Present* moved you a step forward on your path of healing, please take a moment to write a brief review—reviews *truly* help grateful authors reach wider audiences and form growing communities of mutual trust—in love.

DO YOU WISH TO MEDITATE MORE?

Are you ready *and* willing to boost your daily spiritual practice?

The full-length, 28-minute meditation, *One Moon Present Breathwork Meditation* has been crafted under the auspices of Spirit and imbued with a clear intent of helping you honestly detect, lovingly address, and gently release any negativity in your life.

You can get the meditation at this link:

omp.meditation.studioblest.com.

Love Yourself Through series

If you seek healing in your life and are looking for a practical account from the trenches of somebody else's expansion that may inspire you to take your next steps, *Love Yourself Through* is one such report. Its formula continues where *One Moon Present* left off. Check out the series on **loveyourselfthrough.com**, where an ever-growing compilation of transparent, personal stories are shared, working in conjunction with the five practical tools of One Moon Present.

LOVE YOURSELF THROUGH SERIES

Love Yourself Through is a series of direct, hands-on workbooks with clearly defined tools, daily tasks, and goals. An ancient breathwork technique as well as other earth-grounded modalities are the integral ingredients to a conclusive formula called One Moon Present that will transform your life within a single moon cycle. With a potent collection of inspirational stories as the main core of the *Love Yourself Through* books, and a practical, step-by-step guide, you will feel inspired and confident to address and recast blocked feelings or suppressed emotions, whether fear, anger or sadness. Revolutionize your life and experience well-being, health, joy, peace, and love every day—as a rule—not as an exception.

"Borut Lesjak is amazing and so are his gifts! He speaks his truth with pure love and first-hand experience, bringing to us the

compassion and mission of a true healer striving to benefit humanity. He gets to the point and shares what works!"
—*Randi Maggid, vibrational shaman, breathwork healer & author*

lyta.studioblest.com

Ink by Star series

If you enjoy absorbing lightning-quick, quantum bursts of soul-based inspiration as opposed to musing on lengthy expositions of mind-based theory, the *Ink by Star* series of *koans to awaken self-love* is right for you! Read more about the series on **inkbystar.com**, where personal break-through healing creations from Lesjak's own *Captain's Log*, *Vision Chart*, and *My Self-Love Journal* are offered in 20 books and 12 box sets—and counting.

INK BY STAR SERIES

Ink by Star is a series of transparent insights into the life and spirit of a human being. Daily, Lesjak created time and love amidst storms of unexpressed emotion with a single-minded purpose: to rekindle his trust in love. Each note is a piece of a self-healing mosaic he collected from a shattered reality on his personal path to inner freedom. Vulnerable and optimistic, Lesjak exposes his earthly musings in the hope he may inspire others to ignite their own self-love and live to the fullest.

Orion

Hard-rocked by life and drowning after being fired from his dream job, getting diagnosed with diabetes, and receiving divorce papers in the mail, intuitive healer and author Borut Lesjak turned the tide and returned to life and love with the magic and soft power of a breathwork-based healing modality he practices and teaches. Embracing his shadows and learning to be present in self-love, Lesjak found himself mused by star, nature, and wonder to record original inspirational notes. Compiled now in several books, these vignettes have been imagined by light from another realm and inked under the radiance of stars and inspired by the constellation of *Orion*.

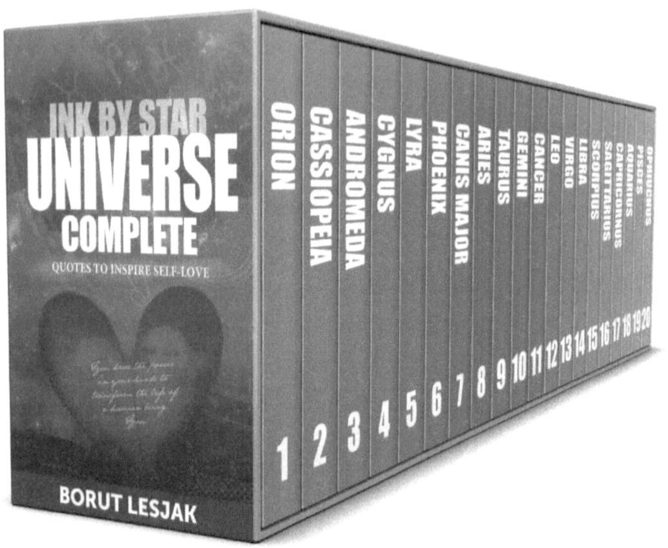

universe.studioblest.com

Mother Earth series

If this book brings joy and healing to your life, discover other soft and loving books—for your children! Visit **motherearthseries.com** and explore the Mother Earth healing series. Can it inspire your kids or dear ones to trust in love, like the Snowflake?

MOTHER EARTH SERIES

A series of seven intertwined wonder tales that dance around the central story of *The Snowflake*. Each story offers a piece of the whole, as the natural elements of snowflake, cloud, wind, sun, tree, river, and snowman all contribute to the healing of Mother Earth.

The Snowflake

The Snowflake is a children's book dipped in the frost magic and snowy enchantment of the winter landscape. As she falls from the sky, the Snowflake becomes separated from her sisters and is blown into an adventure that challenges her to face the world with trust, grace, and heart. This warming tale is a nature elixir for any kid-at-heart and rekindles living sparks of truth, transience, and wonder.

"*The Snowflake* is an imaginative story by Borut Lesjak that holds as much uniqueness as each and every snowflake. It warms the heart and lifts the spirit as gently as the snow landing on Mother Earth!"

—*David Elliott, author, teacher and healer*

Sen & Sanja series

Sen and Sanja of the Magical Arts and Detective Agency star in yet another fantastic fable of one family's healing, in this series of novels for middle-grade readers. Check out what Sen and Sanja are up to on **sensanja.com** and subscribe for news about forthcoming sequels, free books, and unreleased chapters that even older children will find mesmerizing. What will Sen, Sanja, good Old Miss Moany, and trusty trans-dimensional navigator Gigli encounter as they venture into subconscious realms that boggle the mind and confuse the heart?

SEN & SANJA SERIES

Sen and Sanja are ordinary siblings, extraordinarily specialized in investigative wizardry. Together they travel through trickster dimensions and solve curious cases demanding advanced use of quantum spells, mind magic, and serious laughter.

Sen, Sanja, and the Cube of Runes

A pair of magical detective siblings navigate dizzy dark dimensions and decrypt an ancient Cube of Runes to reunite with their missing parents.

Sen, Sanja, and the Clock of Mirrors

The MADA team face their time-shifted selves through a black mirror and crack an impossible paradox to save themselves from never having been born.

Sen, Sanja, and the Coat of Dreams

A sinister mist of oblivion pursues the puzzled sibling investigators across a fraying fabric of lucid dreamscapes in an all-out attempt to erase the memory of human race.

About the author

Borut Lesjak is an intuitive healer and author from Slovenia. Since childhood, he has been drawn to grok the mystery of existence. During the vulnerable years of his carefree youth, he awakened to the awareness of death and life, discovering a gift of claircognizance. Life hard-rocked the sensitive adult Lesjak to a state of hopeless haze until he ignited an inner choice to heal himself. Breathwork meditation coupled with creative expression opened his heart and mind to restore his innocence. Grounded by realness larger than life, he found his calling by bringing clarity, compassion, integration, and joy to this beloved planet for all to experience.

After residing and working in Australia, USA, Mexico, and Paris, France, he is now back in Slovenia growing roots with his wife and three children, offering healing work and writing books. He loves to dream, drive, travel, and hike. He is having fun.

You can connect with Borut at **borutlesjak.com** or stalk him on social media. He self-publishes, and personally reads and responds to his email at **borut@borutlesjak.com**.

"Borut Lesjak is a force of nature, and his unflinching, radical commitment to healing, growth and the transformative power of love is brought to life in *The Snowflake*, a gentle tale about the journey towards union and the magic of harmony with the wild world."

—*Sarah Berti, mythmaker, author of the Helix Library Mythos*